an

(POST)CRITICAL GLOBAL STUDIES 1

Edited by
Márcia Aparecida Amador Mascia, Silvia Grinberg
& Michalis Kontopodis

PETER LANG
Oxford · Bern · Berlin · Bruxelles · Frankfurt am Main · New York · Wien

Facing Poverty and Marginalization

Fifty Years of Critical Research in Brazil

**Michalis Kontopodis,
Maria Cecilia Magalhães
and Maria José Coracini (eds)**

PETER LANG

Oxford · Bern · Berlin · Bruxelles · Frankfurt am Main · New York · Wien

Bibliographic information published by Die Deutsche Nationalbibliothek
Die Deutsche Nationalbibliothek lists this publication in the Deutsche National-
bibliografie; detailed bibliographic data is available on the Internet at http://
dnb.d-nb.de.

A catalogue record for this book is available from the British Library.

Library of Congress Control Number: 2016947656

Cover image: Large common room of occupied territory by the Movimento
Nacional pela Luta pela Moradia (photographed by M. Kontopodis).

ISSN 2297-8534
ISBN 978-1-906165-64-2 (print) • ISBN 978-1-78707-046-2 (ePDF)
ISBN 978-1-78707-047-9 (ePub) • ISBN 978-1-78707-048-6 (mobi)

Published by Peter Lang Ltd, International Academic Publishers,
52 St Giles, Oxford, OX1 3LU, United Kingdom
oxford@peterlang.com, www.peterlang.com

Michalis Kontopodis, Maria Cecilia Camargo Magalhães and Maria José
Coracini have asserted their right under the Copyright, Designs and Patents Act,
1988, to be identified as Editors of this Work.

This publication has been peer reviewed.

Printed in Germany

Contents

(Post)Critical Global Studies: A Note from the Series Editors

It is a great pleasure to introduce the book series (*Post*)*Critical Global Studies* with the publication of its first volume, *Facing Poverty and Marginalization: Fifty Years of Critical Research in Brazil*. As Brazil enters a new phase of socio-economic and political turmoil, distinguished representatives of the various critical research traditions from all over Brazil explore the voices and practices of those who are considered powerless: the helpless, the mentally ill, the delinquent, the landless, the "homeless", the voiceless youth, and the indigenous. In parallel, the volume offers an international audience a first-time glimpse into the new theoretical understandings produced by the critical research that has emerged over the last fifty years in Brazil, such as Freireian pedagogics, critical sociology, ethno-mathematics, critical social psychology, and discourse analysis.

We hope that this volume constitutes a first step into establishing a vibrant exchange of ideas between Latin America and the rest of the world on contemporary social issues, so as to explore the possibilities for the local and global social change that is the broader aim of this series.

Márcia Aparecida Amador Mascia,
Silvia Grinberg & Michalis Kontopodis

MICHALIS KONTOPODIS, MARIA CECILIA CAMARGO
MAGALHÃES & MARIA JOSÉ R. F. CORACINI[1]

Introduction: Fifty Years of Critical Research in Brazil

A Long History of Critical Research ...

A long history of poverty, discrimination, colonialism, and struggle for social justice has provided, over the last fifty years, the context for the development of a vast amount of critical scholarship targeting marginalization in Brazil: Freireian pedagogics, ethnomathematics, anthropology, theology of liberation, critical sociology, critical social psychology and discourse analysis. Most of this scholarship has unfortunately been accessible only to the Portuguese-speaking readership until now. The volume you hold in your hands presents, for the first time to an international audience, the novel understandings of critical social research that have emerged in this frame. While Brazil is entering a new phase of financial crisis and socio-political turmoil, distinguished representatives of these various critical research traditions from all over Brazil explore, in original pieces of work, written for an international readership, the voices and practices of those who are usually hardly heard: the so-called helpless, mentally ill, delinquent, landless, "homeless", voiceless youth, indigenous, powerless.

If one would try to create an overview of Brazilian critical scholarship since the 1970s, one would, of course, end up with a very long list of names and references – an endeavor which is beyond the scope of the present book. Without promising an overview, but just a glimpse of this vast intellectual territory, the present volume presents and discusses timely empirical data

---

1   See Notes on Contributors for information on all editors and authors.

within the above-mentioned broader traditions formed during the last fifty years in Brazil. Building on previous publications that explore Brazil in terms of history, economy, education, social dynamics, and racial politics (Brock & Schwartzman, 2004; Hanchard, 1999; Kontopodis, 2009; Reiter, 2009; Souza & Sinder, 2005; Woolcock & Gacitua-Mario, 2008), our volume takes a closer look at its excluded and marginalized people and their everyday lives, experiences, and struggles.

Our edited volume draws on the different schools of critical research that have been generated in Brazil since around 1960. Social and intellectual movements emerged at this time when poverty, illiteracy, and significant deficits in housing and public health prevailed in agrarian communities as well as in the outskirts of large Brazilian cities. These deficits were deeply rooted in the colonial history of the Brazilian state, and created and sustained a huge difference between the richest and poorest. A crucial turn with regard to these issues took place in the years 1961 to 1964, when civil and student associations as well as workers' unions began gaining space and power in a context of intensified struggles for social justice under President João Goulart's government (1961–1964).

These emerging social movements were causes of great concern for the conservative political forces in Brazil and in the other countries of the American continent. It was feared that a shift to the left would take place in Latin America's largest country and a military coup took place in 1964 and aggravated in 1968, under the allegation that there was a communist threat against the state. This led to the dictatorship that lasted until the presidential election of Tancredo Neves, in 1985. After the military coup, freedom of speech and political organization became almost non-existent. Political parties, workers' unions, student associations, and grassroots organizations were abolished or interfered with by the government, and many of their members were arrested, tortured, killed or exiled. All of the media were repressed by censorship. A series of *Institutional Acts* put into practice censorship, political persecution, suppression of constitutional rights, and the repression of those considered opposed to the military regime.

However, this time also marked the commencement of Brazilian critical theory and research. Paulo Freire's (1921–1997) work on *popular education* and on the liberating and empowering pedagogy of the poor and oppressed was central in this context. Paulo Freire stated in 1958 at an Educational Congress in Rio de Janeiro that adult literacy education should be directly related to the everyday life of the workers, and that workers needed to critically understand their reality in order to actively participate in social and political life so that broader social changes could occur. A decade later, the writings of Paulo Freire portrayed the poor as *disadvantaged* and *made poor* by the economic and social relations that oppressed them (Freire, 1970). These writings also portrayed the poor as producers of types of cultures distinct and different from the dominant ones, and as social transformational forces. According to Freire, the liberation needed to be a result of the struggle of the oppressed themselves, or it would not be true liberation.

These discussions on the need for critical engagement as fundamental to personal and social transformation were also the basis for *Liberation Theology*, a counter-movement within the Catholic Church with Leonardo Boff (1938–) as its most well-known representative. *Liberation Theology* set as its objective the transformation of the poor along with the struggle to improve their quality of life (Boff, 1971, 1972). Both *Liberation Theology* and *Freireian pedagogy* were influenced by Marxist thinking and pointed to the centrality of dialogical and dialectical relations for the constitution of human beings, as well as for the establishment of collective forms of organization in the fight against authoritarianism, oppression, poverty, and illiteracy. Both approaches took critical reflective education as a point of departure for liberating praxis. In this frame, by becoming aware of their own history and the current conditions of social, cultural, and economic inequality, human beings could strive towards a revolutionary struggle for liberation, i.e. towards overcoming the dehumanization that inequality and injustice imply. Both approaches revolutionized their relevant areas of scholarship: *Liberation Theology* by conceptualizing a liberating praxis in which religion and ethics were seen as central forces for critical reflection and awareness; *Pedagogy of the Oppressed* by redefining the theoretical and methodological foundations of educational practice on the basis of dialogue and critique, especially with regard to adult literacy.

While the church provided at least some limited protected space for Boff to develop the theology of liberation, in 1964 Freire was arrested, imprisoned for about seventy days, moved from jail to jail, and then forced into exile with his wife and their five children. The seeds for critical research had, however, already been planted. About a decade later, in 1974, moderate forces within the military brought General Ernesto Geisel to the presidency. Geisel initiated the so-called *abertura* (political opening), a series of reforms that gradually allowed limited political organization and local elections. The legal opposition party, the Brazilian Democratic Movement (MDB), began to win important elections, and in 1979 General João Baptista Figueiredo declared a general amnesty for all political crimes since 1964. He also allowed exiles – including Paulo Freire – to return to Brazil. Figueiredo released the last few political prisoners, and official censors finally left the pressrooms and television studios. He also issued guidelines for the formation of new political parties, and for an open election of governors in 1982.

Within this atmosphere of political openness, critical approaches across a wide range of disciplines were introduced. Eni Puccinelli Orlandi introduced the so-called *French School of Discourse Analysis* by Michel Pêcheux in the late seventies (Orlandi, 1976), an important line of critical research that still flourishes in Brazil today. The notion of language as opaque, polysemous, marked by incompleteness and Otherness has been central here (cf. Furlanetto & de Souza, 2006; Coracini, 2007). At the same time, Marxist and critical approaches became dominant in psychology and sociology through the circulation of original and translated words from France or Germany, such as the *Anti-Oedipus* by Gilles Deleuze & Felix Guattari (translated and published in 1976 in Brazil), the collection *Os Pensadores* ("The Thinkers"), which included the translated texts of Benjamin, Horkheimer, Adorno, and Habermas (published in Portuguese by Editora Abril Cultural in 1975, cf. Benjamin et. al., 1975), or the *Groupes, Organizations, Institutions* of Georges Lappasade (translated in 1977).

Furthermore, the socio-cultural psychological school of Lev Semyonovich Vygotsky, Alexei Nikolaevich Leontiev, and Alexander Romanovich Luria provided another significant source of scholarship, primarily through access to translated works from Portugal and the US (cf. Prestes & Tunes, 2012). The book *Psicologia na Educação* by Claudia Davis and Zilma de Moraes Ramos de Oliveira (1980) could be mentioned here as one of the first publications in this direction, which was followed by a long list of scholarly works in social and educational psychology (for an overview cf. Pino & Mainardes, 2000). On these fertile grounds the "psychology of the oppressed" emerged, as pointed out by Ana Bock & Odair Furtado (2006, p. 510):

> The development of political consciousness becomes an important topic, as the influence of Paulo Freire (1921–1997) is sizable during this period. The radical pedagogy, the freedom of teaching, and the pedagogy of the oppressed influenced the practice of psychology and prompted a form of *psychology of the oppressed*. Hence the discovery of Vygotsky, who took consciousness as an object of study, was a high point for the theoretical scholarship to substantiate the academic production. (translated from Portuguese by the editors)

Around the same time anthropologist Eduardo Viveiros de Castro was publishing his first book on so-called *Amerindian perspectivism* (1986), while *ethnomathematics* – a new field of educational research – was emerging (Ascher, 1984; D'Ambrosio, 1985, Ferreira, 1988). This new field of research focused especially on the social, historical, cultural and political dimensions of mathematical knowledge.

The Present Volume: A Glimpse into Brazilian "Margins"

Facing Poverty and Marginalization provides a glimpse on the above-described intellectual territory through a series of critical case studies of present-day marginal social spaces. The volume opens with the chapter "Life at the Landfill: Portraying Exclusion and Resistance in the Documentary *Estamira* by Marcos Prado". By means of discourse analysis, the author Márcia Aparecida Amador Mascia explores how Estamira represents herself as a "woman", as a "mother", as "mentally ill", as "poor", as "living of garbage", as "sexual assaulted", and as "abandoned by her husband". The analysis searches for the moments of resistance in her discourse and explores how Estamira resists within her own schizophrenic world by understanding herself as a unique person and the only one who knows the "truth."

Maintaining the focus on documentary film production, the second chapter "Struggling for Housing: The November 20 Occupation in Porto Alegre" by Denise Comerlato, Jacqueline Britto Pólvora, and Caroline Stumpf Buaes reflects on the production of a documentary film about activist families participating in the National Movement of Struggle for Housing or National Movement of Housing Vindication. The documentary *A Copa dos 20 de Novembro* [*The November 20 Cup*] (2012) was produced through an outreach project of the Federal University of Rio Grande do Sul (UFRGS) together with members of that occupation, affiliated to the National Movement of Struggle for Housing (MNLM), before their eviction from the area to give way to renovation work for the 2014 FIFA World Cup. Following Freireian thinking and critical urban sociological theory, the analysis explores the November 20 Occupation as a *pedagogical* experience towards a different, novel way of living for all people involved – including the university researchers.

Exploring further how "pedagogy" and "education" can be expanded and redefined *in* and *through* the dialogue with social movements, the third chapter "Educating in Itinerancy: Countryside Life and Novel Forms of Schooling" by Isabela Camini and Michalis Kontopodis explores schooling in itinerancy with a focus on the countryside schools that emerged around 1996 in the context of the Landless Rural Worker's Movement (Movimento dos Trabalhadores Rurais Sem Terra or MST) in Brazil. These so-called "encampment schools" ("escolas do acampamento") or "itinerant schools" ("escolas itinerantes") are usually made out of black nylon fabrics, resembling the other tents of the Landless Workers' encampments: they can be constructed, deconstructed, and reconstructed at each new challenge. The encampment school's social function is to educate the children of Landless Workers wherever they may be until they manage to create a permanent settlement. An itinerant school may thus be found in an encampment, on the side of the road, during a demonstration, or in front of a public building. The chapter discusses the simultaneous struggle for schooling and for agrarian reform, initiated by the Landless Workers' Movement, in this context, and the implications with regards to education and pedagogy in general.

The following chapter "Indigenous Children and Identity Politics: Numeracy Practices among the Kaiabi from Xingu, Mato Grosso" by

Jackeline Rodrigues Mendes explores the symbolic and political aspects of the expansion of numerical terminology in the indigenous language by teachers, elders, and community leaders in their attempt to produce an innovative Kaiabi math book. Based on action-oriented ethnographic research carried out over five years with Kaiabi people from the Xingu Indigenous Park in central Brazil, the chapter investigates, in an ethnomathematical perspective, the Kaiabi cultural meaning of "number" within the broader identity politics of indigenous schooling, taking into consideration the long troublesome history of Portuguese, multilingual, and intercultural indigenous education in Brazil.

The fifth chapter "'Special' and 'Normal' in Students' Voices: Meaning Production at a State-Funded School in Campinas" by Ana Luiza Bustamante Smolka, Lavínia Lopes Salomão Magiolino, Elizabeth dos Santos Braga, and Ana Lucia Horta Nogueira takes the reader to Campinas – a large and rather wealthy metropolitan area in the state of São Paulo. The chapter focuses on young people who face violence, poverty, criminality, and other difficulties in their everyday lives. Teachers speak of these thirteen- to fourteen-year old students as students with "special" characteristics and needs; students in turn argue that their way of living is "normal," referring to everyday life situations of violence, stealing, and facing detrimental conditions. Inspired by Vygotsky and Bakhtin, the authors explore these understandings through a semiotic/discursive perspective and examine timely issues related to normativity and heterogeneity in Brazilian urban state-funded schools.

How to reflect indeed on what is "normal" or "special" in contemporary Brazil? The sixth chapter "The Dis-order of Discourse: Young People Confined in CASA (São Paulo) and a Poet Considered Insane in Colônia Juliano Moreira (Rio de Janeiro)" by Maria José R. F. Coracini explores news articles about "in-famous" young people living in the young offender institution CASA ("Centro de Atendimento Socioeducativo ao Adolescente," with "casa" in Portuguese meaning "home"), as well as tape-recorded oral texts by a black woman (Stela do Patrocínio) who lived in a lunatic asylum. The chapter comments on the relationship between *order* and *disorder*, being *famous* and *infamous, exclusion* and *inclusion, power* and *resistance* (cf. "Les Anormaux," Foucault 2001). These dichotomies and polarizations are broken down in order to defend hybridization – which can be seen as essential in the contemporary Brazilian social and political frame.

Moving further into the Brazilian "margins", the seventh chapter "In-Famous Cyberhomelessness: The 'Homeless' Writer Tião Nicomedes" by Elzira Yoko Uyeno analyses the texts posted on the blog "diariotiao.zip. net," by Sebastião Nicomedes, a "homeless" man. The analysis indicates that the figure of a "homeless" person is taken as a *homo sacer* i.e. a man who has committed a crime, is banned from society, and has had his rights as a citizen revoked (Agamben, 1998). The "homeless" person's "crime" lies in not having a residence of his own. However, the symbolic function of writing has the scope of the Lacanian "double movement": first, the "homeless" person is included in the category of "citizens", and then in the context of this relationship, he expresses his resistance redefining to some extent what a "citizen" may be (cf. Lacan, 1966). The cyber-communicator, in spite of living in a situation of extreme poverty, resists and builds his identity, escaping given norms and discursive orders.

The seven case studies referred to above invite the reader to reflect on the relationship between *social* science and *social* movements as well as on the arbitrary boundaries between so-called "scientists" and "marginalized people". Instead of writing an epilogue, in the final chapter of the volume, Michalis Kontopodis addresses these issues through a poetic ethnographic narration by taking the word "movement" in its various meanings (i.e. movement in space, emotionally moving, social movement and movement of thoughts). "Youth 'in Movement' in Contemporary Brazil: Sharing Intense Moments with José, Carlos, Raquel, and Werá Mirim" invites the reader to follow four young people in what is a "typical day" for them in the context of a variety of social and political movements developed over the last fifty years in Brazil (in particular: the Landless Workers' Movement, indigenous movements, movements for the education of urban workers and/or "homeless" people, and movements for urban housing for all). This final chapter brings together the themes of the volume presented above by exploring the affective dimensions of Otherness and social justice and by sketching an "outside" politics that moves beyond "macro-" and "micro-" political engagement (cf. Stephenson & Papadopoulos, 2006).

Facing Poverty and Marginalization proposes original theoretical tools and arguments that can inspire social-scientific discussions on facing poverty and marginalization not only with regard to Brazil, but also in other parts of the world. We are interested in achieving broader theoretical as well as socio-political contributions, and hope that this volume constitutes the first step in establishing a vibrant exchange of ideas in the years to come among students, researchers, and specialists in fields such as sociology, social psychology, critical theory, education, social inquiry, social work, social policy, and international development.

Acknowledgements

We are immensely grateful to many colleagues from quite different places, as well as numerous research groups in Brazil, who assisted us in completing this book over the past five years. It is quite impossible to mention all their names here and we would like to apologize for that. We owe a special debt in particularly to Ana Bock, Marisol Barenco, Norval Baitello, Maurício Canuto, Claudia Davis, Achilles Delari-Junior, Johannes Doll, Wanda Maria Junqueira de Aguiar, Jader Janer, Erineu Foerste and Gerda-Margit Schutz-Foerste, Nadia Lebedev, Angela Lessa, Ana Lopes, Maria Cristina Meaney, Gilton Mendes, Jessica Santos, Wellington Oliveira, Rita Marisa Ribes Pereira, Vera M. Ramos de Vasconcellos, and most importantly, to Fernanda Liberali and Bernd Fichtner. We cannot thank enough all the authors for their patience through the various steps involved in putting this volume together, Alessandra Anzani from Peter Lang for her kind collaboration, and Jessica Walsh for her great patience in editing our texts in English. We would also like to thank Penny Jane Burke and Kate Hoskins from the University of Roehampton in London, as well as Dimitris Papadopoulos from Leicester University, for their feedback on earlier versions of the manuscript. The book is devoted to our dear colleague Elzira Yoko Uyeno, who passed away before the publication was completed.

References

Agamben, G. (1998). *Homo sacer: Sovereign power and bare life*. Stanford: Stanford University Press.

Ascher, M. (1984). Mathematical ideas in non-western cultures. *Historia Mathematica*, 11(1), 76–80.

Benjamin, W., Horkheimer, M., Adorno, T. W., & Habermas, J. (1975). *Textos escolhidos. Coleção "Os Pensadores" Vol. 48* (Trans. & Eds Z. Loparic & O. B. Arantes Fiori). São Paulo: Abril Cultural.

Bock, A. M. B., & Furtado, O. (2006). História das relações entre o marxismo e a psicologia no Brasil. In: A. M. Jacó-Vilela, A. A. L. Ferreira & F. T. Portugal (Eds), *História da psicologia: Rumos e percursos* (pp. 503–513). Rio de Janeiro: Nau Editora.

Boff, L. (1971). *O Evangelho do Cristo cósmico. A realidade de mito e o mito de uma realidade*. Petrópolis: Vozes.

Boff, L. (1972). *Jesus Cristo libertador. Ensaio de Cristologia crítica para o nosso tempo*. Petrópolis: Vozes.

Brock, C., & Schwartzman, S. (Eds) (2004). *The challenges of education in Brazil*. Oxford: Symposium.

Coracini, M. J. (2007). *A celebração do Outro: Arquivo, memória e identidade – línguas (materna e estrangeira), plurilinguismo e tradução*. Campinas: Mercado de Letras.

D'Ambrosio, U. (1985). *Socio-cultural bases for mathematics education*. Campinas: Mimeo.

Davis, C., & de Oliveira, Z. (1980). *Psicologia na educação*. São Paulo: Cortez.

Delari, J. A. (2010). Lev Vigotski: Bibliografia comentada: Traduções publicadas no Brasil (1984–2010). *História da Pedagogia, 2*, 76–90.

Deleuze, G. &, Guattari, F. (1976). *O Anti-Édipo: Capitalismo e esquizofrenia* (Trans. G. Lamazière). Rio de Janeiro: Imago.

Ferreira, E. S. (1988). *The teaching of mathematics in Brazilian nature communities*. Campinas: Mimeo.

Ferreira, M. C. (2004). Análise de discurso e psicanálise: Uma estranha intimidade. *Correio da APPOA, 131*, 37–52.

Freire, P. (1970). *Pedagogia do oprimido*. Rio de Janeiro: Edições Paz e Terra.

Furlanetto, M. M., & de Souza, O. (Eds) (2006). *Foucault e a autoria*. Florianópolis: Insular.

Hanchard, M. (Ed.) (1999). *Racial politics in contemporary Brazil*. Durham: Duke University Press.

Kontopodis, M. (Ed.) (2009). *Culture and emerging educational challenges: A dialogue with Brazil, Latin America*. Berlin: Lehmanns Media.

Kontopodis, M. (2012). *Neoliberalism, Pedagogy and Human Development: Exploring Time, Mediation and Collectivity in Contemporary Schools*. London and New York: Routledge/Taylor & Francis.

Lacan, J. (1966). *Écrits*. Paris: Éditions du Seuil.

Lacerda, F. Jr. (2013). Capitalismo dependente e a psicologia no Brasil: Das alternativas à psicologia crítica. *Teoría y Crítica de la Psicología* 3, 216–263.

Lapassade, G. (1977). *Grupos, organizações e instituições* (Trans. H. A. Mesquita). Rio de Janeiro: Francisco Alves.

Orlandi, E. P. (1976). O verbo e a voz: uma forma de análise. *Estudos Linguísticos*, 1(1), 37–54.

Pino, A. S., & Mainardes, J. (2000). Publicações brasileiras na perspectiva vigotskiana. *Educação & Sociedade*, 21(71), 255–269.

Prestes, Z., & Tunes, E. (2012). A trajetória de obras de Vigotski: Um longo percurso até os originais. *Estud. psicol. Campinas*, 29(3), 327–340.

Reiter, B. (2009). *Negotiating democracy in Brazil: The politics of exclusion*. Boulder, CO: First Forum Press.

Stephenson, N., & Papadopoulos, D. (2006). *Analysing everyday experience: Social research and political change*. London: Palgrave Macmillan.

Souza, J., & Sinder, V. (Eds) (2005). *Imagining Brazil*. Plymouth: Lexington.

Viveiros de Castro, E. (1986). *Arawete: Os deuses canibais*. Rio de Janeiro: Jorge Zahar/ ANPOCS.

Woolcock, M., & Gacitua-Mario, E. (Eds) (2008). *Social exclusion and mobility in Brazil*. Washington: World Bank.

MÁRCIA APARECIDA AMADOR MASCIA

1. Life at the Landfill: Portraying Exclusion and Resistance in the Documentary *Estamira* by Marcos Prado

Introduction

The need for mapping poverty in Brazil is urgent, as it is understood that poverty has social effects on everyone, including those who are not in a state of poverty. Poverty is responsible for the main issues that affect our daily lives, from violence to illiteracy. As researchers, we should raise social problems and bring them into discussions at conferences, and in articles and books. This chapter therefore aims to present an analysis of a Brazilian audio-visual documentary called *Estamira* (Prado, 2006). This is part of a broader project called "(In-)famous Voices: Discourses of Exclusion and Resistance" (see also Coracini, this volume; Uyeno, this volume) which in turn is part of a national project entitled "The concept of family and poverty on the streets: a critical analysis of the Brazilian context". My sub-project had in these contexts the aim of attending to the voices of doubly excluded subjects: those living in poverty with a disability or mental illness.

In a similar mode, João Biehl (2005), describes in his book "VITA Life in a zone of social abandonment" in detail the life of a "mentally ill" woman, Catarina, living in a rehabilitation center and psychiatric clinic near the city Porto Alegre, the capital of Rio Grande do Sul State, in Brazil, where the "unwanted", the "mentally ill", the "sick", and the "homeless" are left to die, but before dying, they experience a social death, being "literally" abandoned by the world. Whilst Estamira does not live in a rehabilitation center and psychiatric clinic, she is a woman, poor, and considered "mentally ill" in the same way as Catarina.

While Biehl follows an ethnographic approach, the methodological framework I will employ below is that of French Discourse Analysis (FDA). In brief, discourse analysis requires an examination of the socio-historical context within which the discourse is constructed followed by a micro-analysis of the texts. For Foucault, power does not apply only to macro-relations, but also (and mainly) to micro-relations in people's daily lives. Power is subtly spread in micro-relations, and where there is power there is also resistance (Foucault, 1980). Based on this idea the author analyses the lives of "marginalized" people as resistance. Following this approach, my analysis focuses on the ways that Estamira, the main character of the documentary and my subject of analysis, represents herself as "woman", as a "mother", as a "mentally ill" person, as a "marginalized", as "getting her income from the landfill", as a "sexually assaulted woman", and as "abandoned by her husband", as we will see below. This leads us to consider the inextricable relationships between subject, discourse, and socio-historical conditions on the one hand, and power, knowledge, and resistance on the other.

Theoretical Background: French Discourse Analysis

The most significant contribution of French Discourse Analysis (FDA) to linguistic theory lies in combining text analysis with social and ideological analysis. While Althusser's theory of ideology (1971) is considered to be the basis of this approach to discursive analysis, it has been Pêcheux (1982, 1983, 1988), who established the so-called "French Discourse Analysis" (FDA). Pêcheux interprets the subject as constituted by discourse and, therefore, as interweaved by ideology and unconsciousness that the subject does not control. The discourse is viewed beyond its merely linguistic forms and as actually deriving from its socio-historical context. The description of the social-historical context, also referred to as "conditions of production of discourse", aims to put the social representations into focus, as well as to describe the space occupied by subjects in the discursive production.

Viewing the subject as constituted by discourse implies the conception developed by Pêcheux and Fuchs (1975) about the double illusion in which the subject as well as the discursive meaning are inscribed: the first is the deception of the origin of discourse, and the second is the illusion that there is only one possible meaning i.e. truth. From this perspective, the subject is incapable of "consciously" transforming the world; she can provoke changes, but does not have control over the meanings of these changes. Or in other words, the subject can resist, but she cannot know, in advance, the effects of this resistance, as we will see with the analysis of Estamira's discourse.

The first step for a discourse analysis is to set out the social-historical context. After contextualizing the production of a certain discourse, the analyst concentrates on the characteristics of the discourse. Discourse is characterized as possessing constitutive heterogeneity, which implies that engaging in discourse analysis is, fundamentally, trying to find the inter-discourses that are at the center of a particular discourse.

The Context: Rio de Janeiro and the Documentary

My analysis below takes into account excerpts of Estamira speaking in the documentary. It is necessary to contextualize these excerpts by presenting a summary of the documentary and how the images are shown. The documentary is situated in the broader contrast between the extremely "rich" and the extremely "marginalized" people, living next to each other in the same cities, especially in metropolises such as São Paulo and Rio de Janeiro in Brazil. The documentary focuses in particular on the deprived part of the population, as it explores the lives of those who make their living from the landfill. But the garbage is from the wealthy people that live in Rio de Janeiro. Rio de Janeiro was during some time the capital of the country, before the capital moved to Brasília in the sixties. Today, it is considered one of the most beautiful cities of Brazil, the city of Carnival, of wonderful

beaches, of cultural exhibitions, but also the city of severe social problems –
poverty, violence, drug trafficking – amongst others.

Given the above, it is not surprising that Rio has one of the largest
landfills in Brazil – Gramacho – the metropolitan landfill where the documentary was shot. The site is away from the city and it receives more trash
every day than any other landfill in the world: 7,000 tons of garbage arrive
daily, making up 70 per cent of the trash produced by Rio de Janeiro and its
surrounding areas. This landfill is visited every day by people who work as
pickers (catadores). These *catadores* work in the garbage, collecting and selling scrap metal and recyclable materials. They established a community (the
favela of Jardim Gramacho) around the landfill, which is now home to over
13,000 people who are entirely dependent on the trade of recyclable materials.
They have their own association (ACAMJG, the Association of Recycling
Pickers of Jardim Gramacho) for purposes of political representation. The
community has created a decentralized system of recycling collection in
neighboring municipalities: the creation of a recycling center and profes-
sional recognition of the *catador*, enabling *catadores* to be contracted for their
services; the creation of a 24 hour medical clinic; and the construction of
a daycare center and a skills training center. Today, roughly 3,000 *catadores*
work on the landfill (although only 1,752 are officially registered), removing
200 tons of recyclable materials each day. They have extended the life of the
landfill by removing materials that would have otherwise been buried, and
have contributed to the landfill having one of the highest recycling rates in the
world. In 2010, another documentary was launched about Jardim Gramacho
and the *catadores*, *Lixo Estraordinário* (*Waste Land* in English, Walker, 2010),
which thematized the workers' rights of the *catadores*, by collaborating with
Brazilian artist Vik Muniz, who used the trash they sort to create portraits
of the pickers. The documentary was nominated for an Oscar in 2011.

The documentary *Estamira*, however, interested me for the project
described above because it tells the story of a woman, narrated by herself.
Her words interest me; the way she talks about herself, about her place in the
society, her lifetime, her body, and her mind. As this is a documentary, the
story is supposed to be real. Estamira is a rare, strange, and strong name.
The documentary follows the life of this woman as she looks at the world
through her job in the landfill in Rio de Janeiro. In 2000, when Marcos

Prado, one of the directors, was taking photographs at the Gramacho waste disposal, he met Estamira for the first time. She told him that she had a mission "to tell the truth". She then asked him what his mission was. As he could not answer, she announced: "your mission is to reveal my mission". The director accepted her prophecy and followed Estamira and her fellows for several years before launching the documentary.[1]

After years of filming, the 127-minute long documentary was presented in film festivals in 2004 and finally launched in 2006 under the direction of Marcos Prado, and the executive production of Marcos Paulo and José Padilha. It was screened at several national and international festivals, and was awarded the best documentary at the Rio Festival (2004) and the International Exhibition of São Paulo (2004). It was shown for many months in theaters around the country. The movie tells the story of this 63-year-old woman (at the time the documentary was made, in 2004) who was born into a lower class family, suffered a series of misfortunes and was subjected to various types of domestic abuse. At the age of 12, she was given to a brothel by her grandfather. At the age of 17, a man who met her there became fond of her took and her from the brothel, and they began living together. For the first time, she started having what one could call a more "normal" life. But this man had affairs with other women, and she decided to leave him and move from the city to Brasília, where she met her second husband. She lived for 12 years with him, but he also took lovers. When she left him, she had 3 children.

According to her eldest daughter who appears in the documentary, when Estamira left her second husband, she had a job at a supermarket, but she was raped twice. Following the second rape, she started having hallucinations and developed a psychosis, a kind of schizophrenia in which she became delusional and insane, often blaming God for that. But although she blamed God, in a poetic, eloquent, and philosophical language, Estamira says in the film that she had a mission set upon her to reveal and reclaim

---

1   According to Luis Fernando Gallego, psychoanalyst and curator of the 2008 movie exhibition on Cinema and Ethics in the "setor Cultural da Escola de Magistratura do Fórum do Rio de Janeiro". Posted in <http://www.cinemaemcena.com.br/estamira/blog.asp> [date of access 13/01/13].

the *truth*. With a lost childhood in poor, rural Brazil, tormented loves, marriages and consequent frustrations, she ends up working (and for some time living) in Jardim Gramacho, the large rubbish tip on the fringes of Rio de Janeiro, which she declares she loves.

The documentary starts in black and white with Estamira going by bus to the waste disposal site of Jardim Gramacho. When she gets there, it changes to full color. Throughout the documentary, some parts are shown in black and white and some are shown color. This alternation between black and white and colored images can be conceived as a technique used to give the public a feeling of what it is like to be inside Estamira's hallucinatory body. In the first scene at waste disposal site, pieces of black plastic can be seen flying among vultures. This is followed by Estamira's first statement. The documentary is about Estamira and her *truth* – her representation of herself and the world – through her voice over a backdrop of garbage chaos and can be seen as a testimony of her life. Building on this brief summary of the documentary and the notions of *discourse* and *subject* presented above, I will now turn to the way in which Estamira represents herself on a micro level. This will entail identifying the effects of meanings and pointing out how they appear in the linguistic materiality of three excerpts of her talking in the documentary.[2]

Scene One: Mission

In the following excerpt, we can see how Estamira expresses "her mission":

> My mission, besides being Estamira, is to reveal the truth, nothing but the truth. Capturing the lie and rubbing it in, i.e. teaching them what they don't know – the innocence. There are no more innocent people any longer. There are wise guys in reverse. Wise guys in reverse there are, but not innocent people.

2   All excerpts are taken from the film and were translated directly from Portuguese by the author.

Estamira creates a discourse of resistance. She resists inside her own symbolic world, which is a schizophrenic one. This consists mainly of seeing herself as somebody special, enlightened, and chosen to see things that "ordinary" people do not see and she has a mission to tell others what she sees. From a discursive point-of-view, these images of prophetic discourse manifest themselves with the use of the word "mission", as we see in the excerpt above and which is repeated several times throughout the documentary. She does not have a *life*, but a *mission*, as somebody "chosen", not only to tell, but to *reveal* or to *teach* the truth.

The words *reveal* and *teach* imply a specific relationship between people that is different from the relationship implied by the word "tell". The person who *tells* the truth is an "ordinary" person and the truth is also an "ordinary" matter. On the other hand, when a person *reveals* the truth or *teaches* somebody the truth, a "special" place is occupied by this person in the society: this person is presented as somebody "special", "enlightened" and "chosen" – "different" from the rest of the people. This prophetic meaning, which Estamira assigns herself, can be understood in terms of religious discourse and as opposed to the clinical discourse on her being "schizophrenic". As she cannot stand so many frustrations, losses and abandonment, instead of seeing herself as a multiply "marginalized", she rationalizes her life on the other dichotomous pole: as being somebody "special".

Foucault (2000) explores in his volume "Lives of infamous men", the lives of the "marginalized" people, the "(in-)famous", those whose did not have "fame", destined to pass their lives without leaving traces, but who also resisted in a way. Foucault defines this work as an

> ... anthology of existences. Lives of a few lines or a few pages, nameless misfortunes and adventures gathered into a handful of words. Brief lives, encountered by chance in books and documents. (Foucault, 2000, p. 157)

He justifies his choice of lives studied in this book in the following way:

> This is not a book of history. The selection found here was guided by nothing more substantial than my taste, my pleasure, an emotion, laughter, surprise, a certain dread, or some other feeling whose intensity I might have trouble justifying, now that the first moment has passed. (Foucault, 2000, p. 157)

This is how I am presenting Estamira's speech here, as *emotion, surprise, a certain dread* that emerges through analysing a life that as encountered in documents, a documentary movie, in this case.

Another interesting point of reference in the excerpt above is the word "innocent". "Innocent", in this context is the interlocutor of Estamira's prophetic discourse. It refers to the people to whom Estamira's discourse is addressed: the ones who do not know the truth, and in this way are "innocent". However she subverts the meaning of "innocent" in our society: there are no "innocent" people anymore, rather "wise people in reverse". In the past, there were "innocent" people, as we understand from the use of "no more" and "any longer" in the sentence "there are no more innocent people any longer". These innocent people were transformed into "wise guys". In order to consider herself a "wise" person, she can only consider the others as not "wise", building a term: "wise in reverse".

If one considers this term within the documentary's context, namely the waste disposal site of Jardim Gramacho in Rio, which contrasts to the beauty and wealth of Rio de Janeiro and the rest of Brazil, it could be argued that she is denouncing the social dichotomy that people in Rio live in. The "Gramacho" landfill can be seen as a metaphor for what people have done to themselves in the contemporary society. The people around Estamira are "responsible", are not "innocent", are actually "wise guys in reverse". Only "wise guys in reverse" could construct a world of grandfather's abuses, rapes, poverty, betrayal, and abandonment. Aware of these contradictions, she has a mission: to be a "prophet" of the slums.

Scene Two: Vision

In order to justify her mission, Estamira asserts:

> Me, Estamira, I am the vision of everyone. No one can live without me. No one can live without Estamira. And I feel pride and sadness in this. Because they, the negative offensive astro-bodies, befoul the spaces and desire me. Desire me and befoul

everything. All creation is abstract. All space is abstract. Water is abstract. Fire is abstract. All is abstract. And as such, so is Estamira.

Continuing with the representations of herself, the extract above also manifests how Estamira conceives herself as somebody "different", but in the positive sense of being "special". "Vision" belongs to the same semantic field as "mission" from the previous extract. As she is "chosen", she can see things that so-called "ordinary" people do not. As she has this power, everybody needs her: "no one can live without me". This power is manifested in her discourse dichotomously: she is "proud" and "sad" at the same time. "Proud" because she has this power of seeing everything, but "sad" because she is followed by "the negative offensive astro-bodies" that, possibly, in her mind, are trying to prevent her from "revealing the truth". The word "desire" is the linguistic manifestation of this persecution by "negative astro-bodies": "desire me and befoul everything". It shows her struggle to "save" the world.

In this excerpt, we not only see her representation of herself, but also her conception of creation: we are all abstract creations, "space, water, fire and so is Estamira". Philosophy? Madness? Poetry? Estamira speaks of herself as a "person" in spite of being excluded from the society. In-between reason and madness, her discourse can be read as philosophical, poetic, and deeply plausible – a discourse of resistance. Any utterance takes place within certain "discursive formations" and it is within these discursive formations that meanings are defined as acceptable or not. When people talk, they are not only communicating certain contents, but also stating which discursive formations the meanings, which constitute them, belong to. The same utterance can be interpreted in different ways, as "exclusion" or "resistance", for instance, depending on the discursive formation one belongs to, as exemplified by this analysis.

Scene Three: Religious Discourse

As explained above, Estamira's discourse refers to religious inter-discourse, in particular the Catholic Christian discourse, as can be seen in the following excerpt:

Where in the world have you seen anything like that? A person can't walk on the streets where she lives! Neither work inside the house! And neither in any work place anywhere! Where else Lord ... What kind of God is that? What Jesus is this, who only speaks of war and who does not know anything else! Isn't he himself a punster (trocadilho)? Only for idiots, for wise guys in reverse (espertos ao contrário) ... silly, stupid! Has anyone who ever felt afraid of saying the truth avoided dying? Have they? Has anyone who spent day and night, night and day ... with God in their mouths, has anyone avoided dying? They who did as they were told by the ones from his gang, have they avoided dying? Have they avoided starving? Have they avoided impoverishment? No, no way, no one will change my mind.

Estamira starts this excerpt by referring indirectly to the two rapes she was subjected to on the streets where she lived when she was coming back from her work. According to her older daughter, whilst Estamira was being raped she begged the rapist, screaming "stop, please, for God's sake", and the rapist answered "What God? Forget about God" and continued having sex with her in all of the ways that he wanted and then he said that she could leave. Thereafter, according to her daughter, Estamira revolted and began cursing God. She used to be religious and never had hallucinations, but after being raped for the second time, she became delusional and insane, giving up on and blaming God.

That is why Estamira, in this excerpt, asks herself what kind of God can allow women to be raped on the streets that they live. From a discursive point-of-view, her disappointment with "God" manifests itself with the use of many questions, such as "What kind of God is that?". But she gives the only possible answer herself: the opposite of God, "punster" in her words, which can be understood to mean the "demon". God is a character that cheats people by pretending being "good" but who is actually "evil" and cannot be trusted. Or in other words, only "idiots" or "wise guys in reverse", the ones who are no longer "espertinhos" can trust this kind of "God". In this part of the excerpt, she uses four words and expressions with a similar meaning: "idiots", "wise guys in reverse", "silly", and "stupid". This repetition is a maneuver to emphasize her indignation against "God", a "God" that does not protect people, a God that did not protect her when she needed him, when she asked ... And she finishes the excerpt asserting that "no one will change [her] mind". After all, she is the only one who knows the "truth".

She has totally rejected God in her life and sees humans as responsible for their own fate. Through her words, one can see how and why she rationalizes her life this way: in order to run away from her woes, she resists by being, in her mind, a "special" person, "different" from all others. Her audacity with God shocks, nudges and disturbs religious people. Why? Because Estamira tells the truth that one does not want to learn about oneself. Everybody is part of this society that Estamira dissects in such a raw and direct manner. Estamira is an effect of power, and the same time, she resists it.

Foucault's studies (1972, 1977, 1980) analyse the mechanics of power, how power works in daily struggles – the so-called "micro-physics" of power. According to Foucault, power is not only concentrated in the upper classes, the dominant ones; it penetrates the whole of society, constituting itself as a diffuse bundle of micro-powers in the discourses of daily life. Yet, "[t]here are no relations of power without resistances" (Foucault, 1980, p. 142). In this sense, Foucault's strategy for studying power and resistance does not relate to the subject as an agent of her destiny, but as an "effect" of the contingency, that emerges between discursive formations of power and resistance and within a certain production of knowledge and subjectivity.

That is why Estamira can be seen as a subject of her place, and her time, but also as resistant to them. The documentary *Estamira* provides the point of view of the Other, the "different", the "strange" – which is however at the same time "familiar". In a country, in a state, in a city, Rio de Janeiro, the wonderful city, dipped into a landfill, an ethical landfill, the "Gramacho" landfill can be seen as a metaphor for the contemporary society. Estamira's discourse denounces the social dichotomy in which people in Rio live nowadays. In her own way, she creates therefore a discourse of resistance.

The notion of contingency is relevant for this approach, as I am questioning the intentionality of the subject, relating her to the historical context and therefore not to the motives behind one's actions. I am questioning and de-constructing "agency" problematizing Estamira as a "subject", inscribing her on the power-knowledge relations of her time producing,

> … a form of history which can account for the constitution of knowledges, discourses, domains of object, etc., without making reference to a subject which is either transcendental in relation to the field of events or runs its empty sameness throughout the course of history. (Foucault, 1980, p. 117)

If power emerges in terms of micro-physics, it is also in terms of micro-physics that it is possible to resist. For Foucault,

> discourse is not simply that which translates struggles or systems of domination, but is the thing for which and by which there is struggle, discourse is the power which is to be seized. (Foucault, 1984, p. 110)

In the "Lives of Infamous Men" Foucault (2000) characterizes the way power operates in the modern era: power presents itself as a network of disciplinary techniques bringing into visibility the "ordinary" individual as opposed to the "infamous" ones through training, classifying and normalizing. He captures the exact point when and where power operates through a transitory encounter to make the "un-ordinary" individual "visible". Such lives became visible because they violated the rules of their societies and by violating the rules, they became "in-famous", as Estamira became through the documentary: her life became "visible" and "in-famous".

(In-)Famous (Mis-)Fortunes: Estamira's Resistance

Estamira is a carrier and witness of the ways in which the social destinies of the "poorest" and the "mentally ill" are ordered, in Brazil. Her experience and the experiences of those who live at the landfill are "traversed by the country's structural readjustment, unemployment, malfunctioning public health system, and infamously unequal distribution of wealth" (Biehl, 2005, p. 46).

As Kontopodis (2011, p. 88) proposes, "human subjectivity and societal relations are not given; they can be endlessly transformed in dramatic and unpredictable ways". The same occurs with Estamira, this "(in-)famous woman", who in her own way imposes herself as a "person", despite being excluded from society. Her discourse can be read as poetic, philosophical, mad, and wise – all at the same time. In her madness, she seems to say things that "normal" people won't dare to say, but the things she says are so plausible that they have internal and external coherence. Maybe, this is what she gains by being "insane": the possibility of going beyond boundaries, paradigms, and standards without fear or shame. But the great power of her discourse is that it exposes both sides of Estamira – "insanity" and "reason". Estamira has the power of words, words through which she creates her resistance against the world, the God, the violence, the pain, and the suffering. Her mission is to resist by expressing her indignation so eloquently, and revealing her "truth": this is a world where there are "no innocent people any longer, only wise guys in reverse".

Estamira's subjectivity is constructed throughout the documentary by her constant efforts to communicate, to remember, and to predict the future as a "prophet", trying to preserve something unique in herself. The documentary shows her struggle to find her place in a world where people no longer care to make her words and actions meaningful. According to Biehl (2005), who refers to Fanon (1963), the locus of the colonization of the Algerian people under French imperialism was "not necessarily the political and economic institutions of the colonizer but the consciousness and self-reflective capabilities of the colonized" (Bielh, 2005, p. 16). After negating the other personality and all other attributes of their humanity for a long time, people are forced to ask themselves, "In reality, who am I?" (Fanon, 1963, p. 250). "Whose reality?" answers Fanon, "The one constructed by the colonized".

We can think in the same way about so-called "psychotic patients", like Estamira. For Lacan (1977, p. 216), psychoanalysts should let their patients define their own terms, or to access their own "truth". This is, somehow, what the documentary does: it gives Estamira a voice, an opportunity to tell her "truth". As we listen to her, we see a picture of social life emerging, sometimes agonizing, sometimes uncertain; we see "order" as well as "chaos", as she experiences them, and how this experience affects her body and her inner world. In a similar way, like Stela do Patrocínio and Tião Nicomenedes in the by chapters Coracini (in this volume) and Uyeno (in this volume). Stela do Patrocínio is a black and poor woman, who has been confined to a psychiatric hospital for almost thirty years, for whom "the poems functioned as a kind of catharsis, opening her heart (...) allowing her to confess her suffering", according to Coracini (this volume). As regards Tião, his life was suddenly transformed when he lost his job, his fiancée and was sent to the streets. There, as a "homeless", he started a blog through which his "writing under the virtual support has [transformed into] a symbolic function", the function of "inventing himself and taking responsibility for his life", according to Uyeno (this volume).

If we assume that subjectivity is constructed by symbolic representations that permeate language and other semiotic material provided by social interactions, we can conclude that discursive analysis has contributed to our understanding of her "schizophrenia" as a symptom or as a discursive manifestation of Estamira's subjectivity. "Schizophrenia" is a discursive position and for Estamira, a way to survive, to keep herself alive. If discourse and subject are imbricated, one determining the other, when one analyses a discourse, one is actually analysing the subject that is constructing the discourse, or better, that is constructing herself through the discourse. Instead of just seeing Estamira as a "schizophrenic", we dare to say that "schizophrenia" is a discursive manifestation of her inner part, the breaking out of a new subjectivity, the only subjectivity that she finds is still alive.

Listening to "(in-)famous" voices is important in contemporary Brazil, as is stated in the introduction of this volume. My analysis hopefully contributes to drawing attention to and making sense of the voices of the "excluded" ones. Each of us – readers and researchers – has a moral obligation to use theories and research to denounce oppressive mechanisms, especially those that are invisible, and discourse analysis is an approach that is particularly useful to investigate the relationship between language and power and challenge the ways in which material and symbolic goods are distributed among people. In conclusion, this chapter intended to raise new and unthinkable questions and to encourage readers to still raise further questions about Estamira as well as about themselves. The documentary Estamira consists of listening to the Other. Do you listen to Estamira, or does she listen to you? Her revolt against a "rapist God", against "wise guys in reverse", against the "offensive astro-bodies", against the disappointments, against gender violence, against the waste products on the landfill ... urges me and you to think ... at least ... about us ...

References

Althusser, L. (1971). Ideology and ideological state apparatuses. In: Althusser, L. (Ed.) *Lenin and Philosophy and other essays* (pp. 127–186). London: New Left Books.

Biehl, J. (2005). *VITA: Life in a zone of social abandonment*. Los Angeles: University of California Press.

Coracini, M. J. (this volume). The Dis-order of discourse: Young people confined in CASA (São Paulo) and a poet considered insane in Colônia Juliano Moreira (Rio de Janeiro). In: M. Kontopodis, M. C. Magalhães, & M. J. Coracini (Eds), *Facing Poverty and Marginalization: Fifty Years of Critical Research in Brazil*. Oxford: Peter Lang.

Fanon, F. (1963). *The wretched of the earth*. New York: Grove Press.

Foucault, M. (1972). *The archaeology of knowledge*. New York: Harper & Row.

Foucault, M. (1977). *Discipline and Punish: The Birth of the Prison*. New York: Pantheon.

Foucault, M. (1980). *Power/knowledge: Selected interviews and other writings*. (Trans. and Ed. Colin Gordon). New York: Pantheon.

Foucault, M. (1984). The order of discourse. In M. Shapiro (Ed.) *Language and politics* (pp. 108–138). Oxford: Basil Blackwell.

Foucault, M. (2000). *Lives of infamous men* (Ed. James D. Faubion, trans. Robert Hurley). New York: New Press.

Kontopodis, M. (2011). Transforming the power of education for young minority women: Narrations, meta-Reflection, and societal change. *Ethos*, 39(1), 76–97.

Lacan, J. (1977). On a question preliminary to any possible treatment of psychosis. In *Écrit: A selection* (pp. 179–225). New York: W. E. Norton.

Pêcheux, M. (1982). *Language, semantics and ideology*. London: Macmillan.

Pêcheux, M. (1983). Sur les contexts épistemologiques de l'analyse de discours. *Mot*, 9, 7–17.

Pêcheux, M. (1988). Discourse: Structure or event? In: Nelson, C., & Grossberg, L. (Eds). *Marxism and the interpretation of culture* (pp. 633–650). Urbana: University of Illinois Press.

Pêcheux, M., & Fuchs, C. (1975). *Mises au point et perspectives à propos de l'analyse automatique du discours*. Paris: Didier-Larouse.

Prado, M. (2006). *Estamira* (121 min). Rio de Janeiro: Europa Filmes.

Uyeno, E. Y. (this volume). In-Famous cyberhomelessness: The "homeless" writer Tião Nicomedes. In: M. Kontopodis, M. C. Magalhães, & M. J. Coracini (Eds), *Facing poverty and marginalization: 50 years of critical research in Brazil*. Oxford: Peter Lang.

Walker, L. (2010). *Lixo estraordinário* (99 min). Manaus: Paris Filmes.

DENISE COMERLATO, CAROLINE STUMPF BUAES,
& JACQUELINE BRITTO PÓLVORA

2. Struggling for Housing: The November 20 Occupation in Porto Alegre

Translated from Portuguese by Gabriel Egger Moellwald

When living is a privilege, occupying is a right (graffiti on the facade of the "November 20 Occupation")

Introduction

This chapter aims to shed light on the struggle for housing by analysing the production of a documentary film made by the authors and a broader research team from the Federal University of Rio Grande do Sul with members of the November 20 Occupation, associated with the National Movement of Struggle for Housing (MNLM) – also known as National Movement of Housing Vindication. Since 2007, more than 20 families have lived in this occupation near downtown Porto Alegre. Public authorities removed the families in 2013 to give way to renovations planned for the 2014 FIFA World Cup (Porto Alegre was one of the host cities).

Our work began as an outreach project of the Federal University of Rio Grande do Sul (UFRGS) following requests from members of MNLM who wanted to make a documentary film to keep a historical record of the November 20 Occupation. The main goal was to focus on the people that lived in the Occupation, to show their faces, their families, how they lived, and the way they perceive their reality in an attempt to demystify their story for viewers. The media had portrayed them as invaders and blamed them for the illegality of the residence. Thus, the documentary entitled *A Copa dos 20 de Novembro* [*The November 20 Cup*] (Brunetto & Souza, 2012) also became promotional material for MNLM.

The project was developed using perspectives of "Popular Education" or "Education for the People" ("Educação Popular") – based on the works of Paulo Freire (1981, 1983, 1987, 1992) – understood by Brandão (2006) and Brandão and Assumpção (2009) as work done *with and for* communities, groups, and social movements. This theoretical approach paved way for the learning through shared experiences and dialogue. Vested with political importance, it aimed to contribute to the transformation of social life.

Popular Education was established in Brazil and Latin America during the 1970s and 1980s as an idea that subordinates education – as a social practice – and the project of society and development, to the interests of the people. In this way, education is understood in a much broader sense, and even if it can be instituted in formal courses, it takes place as a political and methodological choice contained in every action of *supporting and collaborating with* the people from lower socio-economic milieus.

According to Paludo (2001), in the 1990s, a wider resignification of the idea of Popular Education occurred in terms of its political orientation. These changes imbued further value to a humane, technical-political education, and occurred in the spheres listed below:

> a) the processes experienced by the organizations themselves, with a large emphasis on the experiences of the subjects in this process; b) autonomy and popular protagonism, that is, the development of subjects' capability of assuming the conditions of their own personal and collective history; c) the process of reconstituting identities through the educational and pedagogical processes, mainly through the study of history; d) the new relationship between education and culture, expressed in an education geared towards daily life and the construction of new ways of life [...]. (2001, p. 205, translated from Portuguese by the authors and G. Moellwald)

As we intend to demonstrate here, the MNLM, represented by the residents of the November 20 Occupation, proposed that every action, production, and meeting should be pedagogical for the following reason: For political subjects to commit themselves to a social movement, they need to identify with each other, and get to know the broader history of their struggle. As a result, they will be able to contribute to social movements whilst maintaining their autonomy. It will enable to deter the possibility of being coopted or patronized by politicians or even entrepreneurs interested in taking advantage of a certain group of people. This was the topic of the first meeting held between members of the university team and the Occupation, as there was a need for a relationship of trust that only time and experience of being and working together could establish. To conclude, what we saw at the Occupation was the construction of a new way of life, a collective struggle to overcome all forms of oppression, be they economic, racial, or gender-based.

To contribute to the education of the residents of the Occupation, several preparatory workshops were carried out for the production of the documentary. By granting access to all of the knowledge involved in the production, these workshops also served to further empower the participants. *Empowerment*, a concept resignified by Freire and colleagues (Freire & Shor, 1986), is understood here as a strengthener of the emancipatory perspective of Popular Education involving the formative, educational and pedagogical aspects of all human relationships (meaning that relationships can also be weakening or unempowering). Contrary to an individualistic or merely psychological perspective, the term *empowerment* in the Freirean sense is understood as a social and political action that exceeds merely activating creative potential, or developing and boosting a person's skills. For Freire and colleagues (Freire & Macedo, 1990; Freire & Shor, 1986), empowerment is always a social and creative act of liberation that unites awareness and freedom: it is the comprehension of reality that empowers the subject/group, increasing their capacity to act in the world.

According to Baquero (2012),

> [E]mpowerment can be understood as emerging from a process of social action in which individuals take hold of their own lives by interacting with other individuals, generating a critical perspective of reality, favoring the construction of personal and social capacity, and enabling the transformation of social relations of power. (p. 181, translated from Portuguese by the authors and G. Moellwald)

Thus, the joint production of the documentary with the November 20 Occupation had a pedagogical aspect that strengthened both the subjects and the collective in their struggle for housing. An important contribution was therefore to enable members of MNLM to carry out their own creative processes through the appropriation of the knowledge and technology involved.[1] It is also worth noting that Popular Education "is founded on a comprehension of human needs beyond material or basic needs" (Paludo, 2001, p. 205). It involves affection, appreciation, participation, knowledge, sharing, and joy. Integral human needs are seen as not mere necessities, but also potentialities that can be strengthened through formative and pedagogical processes and in every action of the social movement. In other words, these elements are apprehended and pursued by the group for its own empowerment. That is why it was necessary for the members of the university team to pay attention to the residents of the Occupation: so that a sense of appreciation and affection could develop between the different groups. Therefore, alongside the work meetings, for the first half of 2010, Members of the university team participated in many festivities and celebrations of the November 20 Occupation.

This chapter is a result of our involvement in the production of the documentary. It sets out a brief history of MNLM, describes the November 20 Occupation, discusses the 2014 FIFA World Cup as a mega event, and presents the accounts[2] of the Occupation's residents with the aim of giving the members of MNLM and the Occupation a voice. The accounts represent the residents' ideas about and perspectives of the struggle, and are based on their lives as they became protagonists of a social struggle. The methodology of action research, as well as the production and data analysis, were based on the principles of popular education as well as on urban sociology – a theoretical field that studies the development of cities, the constitution of groups with distinct social visions to each other, and the disputes for urban spaces.

---

1   Cf. <http://ocupacao20denovembro.blogspot.com/> [date of access: 27/05/16]

2   Accounts used in this text were mostly recorded audio-visually. Some narratives and/or dialogues were registered in writing in field diaries. The use of accounts in this text was authorized by the relevant parties. In order to reference the subjects, we chose to present, in parenthesis, the gender, age and number of their children, when applicable.

History of the National Movement of Struggle for Housing (MNLM)

The history of the social mobilization for the struggle for housing takes us back to the 1950s and the developmental model implemented in Brazil at the time. At the time, the technologization of agriculture caused a massive unemployment of rural workers and attracted the workforce to the cities in a fast process of industrialization, resulting in a predominantly urban population by the 1970s. The extremely fast urbanization that occurred within a few decades caused huge social changes in the country, the phenomenon of *favelization*³ of the cities being one of them. *Favelization* is understood here not only as the irregular occupation of terrains, but also incorporates hazardous housing conditions, including public housing projects. In this sense, the *favelization* of cities corresponds to a generalized decline in the quality of life of their inhabitants. Studies such as the 2010/2011 Habitat Program Report sponsored by the UN, revealed that 28 per cent of the Brazilian population lives in registered *favelas* (Instituto de Pesquisa Econômica Aplicada, n.d.). In this socio-historical context, we find a large number of irregular occupations in idle spaces or in urban areas considered of high physical and social risk. Thus, a significant part of the population has no choice but to live in places far from the benefits offered by the city, such as schools, hospitals, and daycare centers.

The hazardous housing conditions that affect millions of Brazilians are the result of the country's economic and political development model adopted for decades by successive governments. This model is the root of the country's unequal income distribution, which privileges private interests and profitmaking to the detriment of the public and collective interests (Kohara, Uemura, & Ferro, 2012). Starting in the 1970s, Brazil saw also the emergence of a large number of social movements (cf. Kontopodis, Magalhaes & Coracini, this

---

3   *Favelization* is used to designate the process of a place becoming a *favela*. *Favela* is a Brazilian-Portuguese word that may translate as "slum"; Brazilian *favelas* have however a quite distinct structure and organization of life than in other places of the world, cf. Perlman, 2010.

volume). In that decade, the inability to sustain steady economic growth and the use of national reserves to pay foreign debt unleashed a crisis followed by a recession in the 1980s. Unemployment, the increase of rent, and changes in legislation relating to urban land all hampered the establishment of new urban areas. The exhausting of available space in the existing *favelas* led to the collective occupation of urban areas and the constitution of the movements for the struggle for housing (Gohn, 1991).

MNLM was established in July 1990 during the 1st National Meeting of Movements for Housing, with representatives from 13 States.[4] It was the result of the union of several groups and movements following the occupation of large areas and housing projects in urban centers mainly during the 1980s. Along with several agencies, the foundation of the movement had the support of the National Conference of Bishops of Brazil (CNBB), Caritas Institute, and the Union of Popular Movements. Today it is also associated with the Unified Workers' Central (CUT) and connected to the Landless Workers' Movement (MST).

MNLM aims to minimize and ultimately end the housing deficit by stimulating the national organization and articulation of the movements for the struggle for housing. Its members are mostly "homeless" people, evicted tenants, and indebted mortgagees from the urban peripheries who organized and united their struggles for housing and access to the fundamental rights of the city. It is worth emphasizing that the debate on urban reform comprises not only the issue of housing, but also the entire urban context: education, health, economy, work, communication, environment, urban mobility, and human relations.

Thus, MNLM is concerned with many contemporary issues, including socio-environmental ones such as water care, reuse of materials, waste reuse and recycling, ecological and organic production, and the use of alternative energies. It is also concerned with: gender issues, especially regarding the protection of women and children and establishing partnerships with feminist movements and the LGBT community; race and ethnicity-related issues, intersecting with the struggle of the black and

---

4   Information available at <http://mnlm-rs.blogspot.com/> [date of access: 27/05/16]

indigenous movements; and issues relating to capitalist production processes, presenting an alternative proposal based on cooperative work and
the Solidary Economy. MNLM exists in 14 of the 26 Brazilian States as
well as in the Federal District.

MNLM was established in the historical context of the political and
social consolidation of democracy in Brazil after the end of the military
dictatorship in 1984. The 1988 Federal Constitution initiated a debate about
the social function of the city and of property, which came to fruition in the
2011 City Statute. MNLM is one of the major national movements for the
struggle for housing, whose leaders have, over the last few decades, pushed
for the effective implementation of these laws (Buonfiglio, 2007). It has
also demanded the social appropriation of urban centers, understood as
the right to the city. The current urban policy has produced a continuous
process of peripherization and *favelization*, creating settlements increasingly
farther from city centers and lacking minimal infrastructure.

Many urban struggles have been witnessed in Brazil, especially since
2000, as a demonstration of resistance in the face of increasing poverty
and social instability in a neoliberal context. It is worth emphasizing, for
example, the June 2013 protests[5] that were sparked by the increase of transportation fees in São Paulo and spread to the main cities of the country,
becoming notorious on a global level. Likewise, the occupation of buildings in the central parts of towns has intensified in recent years in several
Brazilian capitals such as Curitiba, Fortaleza, Porto Alegre, Recife, Salvador,
Rio de Janeiro, and São Paulo.

The space conquered by an occupation is the foundation of the political struggle for the renegotiation of effective housing and the enhancement
of social equality. Temporary occupations are also carried out, as a way to
denounce the empty spaces and idle buildings in town, be they public or
private.

> Central neighborhoods have the potential to house a large number of residents, given
> that these areas have suffered a decline in population for decades and still contain

---

5   Cf. the documentary produced by TVFOLHA: <https://www.youtube.com/
     watch?v=AMprLfFSGPc> [date of access: 27/05/16]

a large number of empty properties. Nevertheless, projects aimed at the revitalization or revalorization of these areas frequently expel the low-income population. They become victims of "hygienist" and elitist actions [...]. Public authorities should develop instruments for the protection of low-income families in these central areas. Otherwise, expulsion becomes inevitable. (Kohara, Uemura, & Ferro, 2012, p. 14, translated from Portuguese by the authors and G. Moellwald)

Thus, the struggles that take place can bring about the convergence of two public policies for urban space: the reoccupation of city centers – abandoned and devalued in the era of shopping malls – and the need for social housing.

We can observe, in the words of a resident of the November 20 Occupation, an awareness of taking part in a collective action that requires its own understanding:

When someone occupies a green area, or sets up an improvised tent in a park, it means that they are searching for a place to live, in a way that is different from a person who wants to stay on the streets. Even if only symbolically, it is a way of saying that things are not good, that there is a social problem, a lack of housing. Something is wrong, and it is private property, and the concentration of income. In some of MNLM's actions, a group of people living on the bank of a stream get together with people unable to pay the rent, that are being evicted, and they start to organize themselves. Twenty or thirty families get together, they search for idle spaces that have no reason not to be used for housing, especially public areas, but also private areas that have not been used for a long time and that can offer a certain degree of infrastructure for people, with water and not being located in very distant areas. The movement was born with this struggle for housing, but wants much more than that. (Male, 26 years old, translated from Portuguese by the authors and G. Moellwald)

We can also observe in the statement above, that the struggle changed as the activists realized that the struggle for housing was not enough. "The Movement was born with this struggle for housing, but wants much more than that". In order to guarantee the rights of citizens, the MNLM has therefore widened its struggle under the new umbrella of urban reform. In this sense, it is necessary to understand the use of urban space from the perspective of the social movement for the struggle for housing in order to create a more egalitarian city, taking into consideration the needs and interests of various groups of dwellers.

Setting the Scene of the November 20 Occupation

Twenty-three families comprising of more than 60 people occupied an area not far from downtown Porto Alegre, next to a large stadium on the shores of Lake Guaíba, a wealthy space due to its privileged location. Children, teenagers, seniors, women, and men all lived on the site, sharing the halls of the main house and a series of shacks surrounding it. Together, they constituted the November 20 Occupation. The name is a reference to the date of the group's previous occupation in a downtown building in 2006. That occupation lasted only three months. At the start of 2007, the families were evicted with the deployment of a large police force. Following negotiations with city authorities, they were relocated to a new, supposedly temporary space.

At first, there were only ruins of what had once been a halfway house for youth.[6] It was a depredated space, without tiling, flooring or windows, as it had been constantly looted throughout the many years that it had remained abandoned. The house was partially rebuilt and became the main house containing a large room for weekly assemblies, festivities, debates, and all sorts of activities. There was a collective kitchen in the back and two bathrooms in the front. Circling the main house were several shacks, mostly one-rooms that sheltered more than half of the families. Others lived in the main house, with each room sheltering one family. In the main house, there was a space for screen-printing and a cooperative that had already baked bread and had been an outlet for various products that had been produced cooperatively and sold for a low price and/or exchanged with other products. In the yard, a warehouse was used for waste recycling and a water tank served to water the garden. There was also a place for the children's activities.

The Occupation, despite its precarious conditions, was a very well distributed and organized space. The houses had no ceilings or flooring and

---

6 House intended for children and teenagers at risk, whether living on the streets or removed from their families as victims of abuse and/or neglect from their parents. In these circumstances, they are placed under State custody.

unpainted walls, but this was compensated by colorful paintings, graffiti and posters of the struggle. During the day, children played in the yard, women hung clothes on the clothesline, different residents sat around in circles to talk or discuss specific issues. Neighbors of the stadium of Sport Club *Internacional* on one side and a samba school on the other, a large *favela* stood at the back of the terrain. Across from the occupation, on the other side of the avenue, stood a large private religious school and a public nursing home. Right behind these institutions was a hill on which luxury condominiums and *favelas* shared the same territory, despite the conflict, revealing the city's social disparities

At night, the yard became a paid parking lot for people who came to watch *Internacional* matches or to the samba school next door, generating the Occupation's main source of income. The money collected from the management of the parking lot was almost entirely distributed among the collective. The rest went to the people who worked on the activity to pay for personal expenses. Not every resident worked exclusively in the Occupation, although everyone received tasks relating to the organization of the collective spaces and the political struggle itself. These tasks were mandatory and if not completed could lead to expulsion from the Occupation and consequently the MNLM.

Life in the Occupation was difficult in many ways, but it was also full of joy. There were frequent parties, maybe due to the high number of youths. Adults and youths cared equally for the children in a broad social space. The Occupation also protected female victims of violence, abandoned seniors, former "homeless" people that had lost touch with their families, among others that had been excluded from society. What united them was not their history of poverty and violence, but the struggle for Urban Reform and the assurance of human rights.

Below, a resident of the Occupation shares her ideas on the struggle by highlighting a paradox between *invasion* and *occupation*, between *contravention* and *utilization*. These words symbolize two antagonistic positions: that of the economic and political elite, including the police force, who refer to the movement as an *invader* and an *offender*, and that of the MNLM, founded on the idea of *right of occupation understood as the use* of idle urban buildings and terrains, guided by the principle of social well-being.

I am not an invader; I occupy an area that had no social function, an unused space. So, we went and occupied the space to later legalize it. So much empty space for years and they don't do a thing about it. These places only serve for prostitution, drug abuse, that sort of thing, several transgressions. When I tell people outside the Movement about this, they begin to think. Today there are several laws on paper, but there is a long way to go until they actually start functioning. Social injustice is something that makes me very angry. So much empty space, it's all about the money and we're not worth a dime to them. I think that is how they see us. Even if you're a productive person, people see you with other eyes. Being a woman, being black and being poor, is a huge flaw. (Female, 45 years old, mother of two children, translated from Portuguese by the authors and G. Moellwald)

Language itself is a means of building meanings, as can be observed in the statement above. Words are full of significations of our existential reality. Therefore, it is through language that the reflection and elaboration of experience occurs, which is an extremely personal and at the same time profoundly social process (Freire, 1986). In this sense, language is never neutral, but rather carries a certain culturally transmitted perspective of the world, according to class interests of the social group that produces it. In the statement above, the woman affirms that empty space is what produces transgressions, contrary to the perspective of the economic powers and the media, which instead portrays the occupiers as offenders. "These places only serve for prostitution, drug abuse, that sort of thing, several contraventions". Therefore, it is necessary to critically analyse the impositions of language and the cultural domination of the more privileged segments, those that occupy the positions of power in society.

2014 FIFA World Cup: Mega Events and Democracy

In 2010, another factor entered into play: the threat of eviction due to a project to expand the area of Sport Club Internacional in partnership with the City as part of the preparations for the 2014 FIFA World Cup. The plan was to build a hotel and a recreation area in the space of the Occupation:

There is the Cup project, but there are also the projects of families that need housing, and that's what they (the authorities) need to realize. We don't know when we will have to leave and what will happen to the twenty-three families that live here. (Male, 33 years old, translated from Portuguese by the authors and G. Moellwald)

With the 2014 FIFA World Cup and 2016 Olympic Games taking place in Brazil, the process of evicting the low-income population from central areas grew harsher, given that the construction work needed for the mega events is guided by a business case that always overrides the social rights of the population.

Promoting the "hygienization" of areas of high visibility during the games is a neces-sary condition for creating the "post card city". These actions, common in host cities of mega event, are part of strategic urban plans based on conceptualizing the city as an enterprise. That is, efficient cities for financial investments and safe for sponsors, in which extreme poverty and social conflicts cannot exist in order not to maculate the presentation of the product on sale. (Kohara, Uemura & Ferro, 2012, p. 19, trans-lated from Portuguese by the authors and G. Moellwald)

In the case of Porto Alegre, the construction work planned for the 2014 FIFA World Cup caused large-scale evictions throughout the city[7] with-out adequate relocation plans for the evicted families. Moreover, accord-ing to the Presidency of the Republic's General Secretariat (Secretaria Geral da Presidência da República, 2014), more than 90 per cent of evic-tions affected low-income families that earn up to three minimum wages.[8] The evictions were all carried out without the necessary dialogue with the directly affected population. In the words of a resident of the Occupation:

The debate now is that with the Cup, there will be economic and social hygien-ization, that they will wipe (this Occupation) clean, that they won't let the car-roceiros[9] move around the city with their carts. The important thing is to raise awareness and have a debate so people think about what they want for the

7   See: <http://comitepopularcopapoa2014.blogspot.com.br/> [date of access 27/05/16]
8   In 2016, three minimum wages amounted to around US$ 659.
9   *Carroceiros* are individuals who work informally collecting recyclable waste using carts as means of transportation.

city. Now private property will come here and build a hotel. Why don't people think that the space could have other uses, especially because it is a public space. Why don't they build a public hotel for those in need, without trying to make a profit? This would be a way to solve not only the Cup problem, but also a city problem. (Male, 26 years old, translated from Portuguese by the authors and G. Moellwald)

A mega event such as the World Cup, or the Olympic Games, has multiple effects on host cities. This could also be an important opportunity to "raise the debate so people think what they want for the city", according to the account above. There are several positive effects involved, such as the demonstration of civility and local hospitality on a global level, having the cities and the country displayed on the international stage. On a local level, there are changes in city infrastructure due to the urban transformation of certain zones and both the short and long-term generation of jobs. These are all anticipated and desired effects in cities that host major events, and many leave their mark on social life (McDonogh, 2002).

Other cities have also experienced the reality of a mega event and its ugly consequences for the poor. The most evident side effect – and fastest to occur – is the removal of part of these populations from areas earmarked for the building of mega-structures for the event. After the improvements are made, the value of these locations increases and rates become unviable for the low-income population. The example of the 1992 Barcelona Olympics is notorious, with the construction of a set of apartment buildings named the Olympic Village with the intention of later selling them at reduced rates. However, these apartments sold far above market prices as a consequence of real-estate speculation on the area (Nello, 1997).

Another consequence of these restructuring operations is the dislocation and consequent replacement of small local shops by large companies or major brand chains adapted to the taste of the international tourist. The same happens in the food sector, hotels and even entertainment, with new, more expensive movie theaters. This phenomenon is known in sociology as *gentrification* (Smith, 1996), understood as the increase in value of a given urban space. Such phenomenon can involve the removal of the traditional residents from the location, improvement of the area and consequent increasing the real estate value. According to Ribeiro (2014),

> [M]ega events such as the World Cup or the Olympic Games are organized by giving priority to meet the demands of organizing committees, sponsors, and urban entrepreneurs from the cities involved [...]. That is also the reason why decisions concerning the city are not made from the perspective of considering its totality, but in a fragmented way, with interventions that serve the interests of construction companies much more than the common well-being of its inhabitants. [...] The recurring jargon in government reports and consulting firms, the "revitalization of degraded areas", sidesteps the growth of high-level real estate exploitation to the detriment of solving the crucial problems of underprivileged distant areas. (p. 14, translated from Portuguese by the authors and G. Moellwald)

It is obvious that the organizing committees of mega events consider the city a commodity and not the living space of its citizens, which justifies large investments in potentially profitable areas, the removal of low-income populations from these regions, and the complete disregard for the overall interests of the city.[10] Moreover, mega events cause an increase in expenditure, enabling corruption and overbilling (Curi, 2013). Unfinished, poorly executed, overbilled constructions and reports of corruption involving politicians and sports managers have caused people to question the legitimacy of the heavy use of public resources for mega events.

Of course the problem of lack of housing and the fulfillment of human rights in Brazil predates the mega events in the country. However, it is undeniable that these events highlighted the political dispute around different conceptions of development, modernity, and progress that affect society as a whole. On such occasions, economic and political power, as well as the urgency to fulfill a schedule, reduces the exercise of citizenship, further hampering the construction of a democratic society.

---

10   Information taken from the following web resources: <http://rio.portalpopulardacopa.org.br/> [date of access: 27/05/16]; <https://comitepopulario.wordpress.com/> [date of access: 27/05/16]; <http://www.apublica.org/wp-content/uploads/2012/09/dossic3aa-megaeventos-e-violac3a7c3b5es-dos-direitos-humanos-no-rio-de-janeiro.pdf> [date of access: 27/05/16]

Coexistence and Dialogue as Methodological Foundations for Action Research

In March 2010, a few months after the MNLM Occupation was notified of its removal from the location, a group, formed initially by a research-professor along with four students at UFRGS, began their outreach project with the aim of producing the documentary. Soon, two other professors and two more students joined the group along with other collaborators. The first step was insertion in the field, with the participation of the UFRGS group in all of the Occupation's activities. These activities involved coexisting on a daily basis – getting to know the work developed in the space, the movement of its residents, the way it was organized – and participating in meetings, assemblies, and festivities. This demanded the presence of the UFRGS group, or at least part of it, in the Occupation for around three days a week, which generated a different presence in the space. Residents began deeply debating what they wanted from the documentary and how they wanted it made.

A basic condition for the production was that the documentary had to be made within a genuine partnership with the UFRGS collectively. The residents of the *Occupation* wanted to be coauthors, to acquire the technical expertise involved in all stages of production, as well as the technological resources (a video camera was purchased for the Occupation). Thus, during the months of May and June, a series of joint workshops were held (including photography, cinematography, art direction, scriptwriting, directing, and editing) with the participation of several other experts – journalists, photographers, and video producers – from UFRGS, including residents of the Occupation as well as many other professionals, either independent or associated to the UFRGS League of Human Rights.

Recording sessions took place in July, when a certain degree of intimacy had already been established among all participants and after the construction of a relationship of mutual trust. Interviews were carried out with 15 people and images were made with 51 of the 60 residents. The documentary *A Copa dos 20 de Novembro* [*The November 20 Cup*] was finished in 2012, two years after starting to work on it. This period saw the participation of 20 professionals and collaborators and the support of several institutions and people connected to social struggles.

Coexisting with a group belonging to an organized social movement was a permanent challenge for our (academic) logic of production, and in particular of the organization of time and daily routine. For the group that lived in the Occupation, it was not only a matter of discourse on the access to rights and new ways of life, it was about enforcing their ideals: shared spaces, collective decisions and cooperative work. As a critical view of capitalist society, private property, labour exploitation, and individualistic and predatory values, they proposed a counterpoint, an alternative, a radical search for coherence between thinking and acting in the struggle for a fairer, more democratic society.

Our introduction to the Occupation also meant committing to the struggle for social change. This was the point of convergence: the time and space of the *Occupation* and its eviction meant that the actions of MNLM crossed paths with studies on urban sociology and Popular Education, more specifically on the experience of the constitution of personal identity as well as of politically active collectives. The different groups involved in the production of the documentary about the November 20 Occupation, by forming an articulate network with a common goal, also produced a pedagogical space. Comprehending other's realities is not a simple task. It is necessary to coexist, to engage, to be open to other ways of seeing and living the world. Coexistence demanded that the researchers in this process of collective production develop their listening abilities, to learn the time and movement of residents, given that researchers were inside their lives and homes.

This experience was only possible because it was anchored in the principles of Popular Education. In other words, it sought to remove all paternalist attitudes, as well as any verticality in the relationship between participating groups, which also meant recognizing the different implied social positions. Popular Education is founded on a political-participative dimension, in which social intervention aims, through dialogue, to evoke the expression of the existential experiences of participants so these can be (re)signified, amplified, and complexified, empowering the subject and the group in the quest for social change. Therefore, social interaction is a central element in the emancipatory processes. We are dialogical beings, formed in the world, in the concrete reality of relations through which we give life meaning (Freire, 1987).

Within this framework, we can understand the importance of the dialogue below, which took place during an assessment meeting. We can observe that university researchers were also challenged to build new conceptions of reality.

RESEARCHER: I don't understand why you want to negotiate another place to live, and why you want to go downtown in particular. Abandoning the space of the Occupation, you will let them build a hotel in this spot.

MNLM MEMBER: Yes, but what can we do? City hall will remove us. We also want to go downtown where everything is a little easier. When we were in the building downtown, people came from the countryside and got together there. It was much better.

RESEARCHER: Yes, but if you leave, the whole city will lose this space, which could have another use.

MNLM MEMBER: If it's the whole city that loses, why aren't you also here? Why don't you stay here? We won't stay just to become cannon fodder.
(Interview excerpt, translated from Portuguese by the authors and G. Moellwald)

There is no dialogue without love, without openness: wanting, knowing, and offering to be known. Knowledge here mixes with experience, for it is knowledge gained from coexisting, from being together and acting together within a relationship of trust that only time and coexistence are capable of building. Affection can be understood as the possibility of being with the other, open and welcoming of the differences between subjects. Thus, for Freire, "love is an act of courage; [...] the act of love lies in committing to its cause – the cause of its liberation. However, this commitment, because it is passionate and affective, it is dialogical" (1987, p. 45).

At the Occupation, we participated in meetings, debates, parties, and collective actions. At the university, members of MNLM participated in classes, seminars, and lectures. A reciprocal exchange was built based on asymmetric relations that acknowledge the different ideas/experience/cultures of both parties. Here, a new collective approach was carried out in the different participating groups, allowing for bold actions and the creation and development of mutual trust. Many of these cooperative and liberating experiences occurred in meetings, as well as passionate confrontations (as presented in the dialogue above between researcher and MNLM member), in other words, conversations that seek to problematize a reality/situation in order to overcome it.

Empowerment and Struggle

Listening to the voices of the subjects involved in the struggle for housing was necessary for the researchers to understand the process of action-reflec-tion-action as brought to us by Freire (1987, 1992), in which, by changing the world, the subject is also changed. Through collective action-reflection, in the interaction between participants, members of MNLM produced new conceptions of the world that, in addition to generating new actions, helped them constitute themselves as protagonist subjects in the struggle for housing and urban reform. Thus, we further analyse the increase of empowerment and the valorization of the role of each person in the struggle.

> I am from Santana do Livramento, on the border with Rivera (Uruguay). I came from there when I was 11 years old and since then I've lived in several places here in metropolitan Porto Alegre and here I am now. When I was 14, I left home and went to make a living, having many housing problems. I studied, got married, divorced, then left a slum and went to occupy, fight for urban reform, for the idea that we also have the right to live in a better place, to have access to recreation, culture, and everything else that exists downtown, because outside (on the periphery), there isn't much we can do. The only thing my children did was play ball in the middle of the street because where I lived there was no playground, nothing. I had a neighbor friend that invited me to occupy the Caldas Junior building and I went. This was my first contact with the movement, I started getting to know it and learning to like it, it was something new for me. This gave me strength to fight for our ideals. (Female, 45 years old, mother of two children, translated from Portuguese by the authors and G. Moellwald)

The struggle for urban reform is appropriated here by the protagonist when she says: "I went to occupy, fight for urban reform, for the idea that we also have the right to live in a better place, of having recreation, culture". The person has thus become aware that she has the right to struggle for a better life. This person should have the access, as every citizen should, to public goods and services, such as culture and recreation offered in the central parts or in other areas of the city with more urban infrastructure and services. By acknowledging themselves as historical beings, inscribed within a temporality, men and women create and transform themselves through reflection and the construction of meaning for their existences because they are aware of their activity in the world.

Narrating and sharing experiences are powerful tools in the struggle to acknowledge and overcome the historical and concrete dimensions of a reality that subordinates and abuses human dignity. For it is when critical perception is established, within the action itself, that an atmosphere of hope and trust develops, leading the subjects, individually and collectively, to work hard to overcome the situation of oppression (Freire, 1987).

> I was very shy. I didn't speak to anyone, I couldn't speak. I was embarrassed around people ... And in the building, we lived with different people. They weren't families, they were different people and we had to learn to coexist. In these four years that we lived there, we made our own family, it was a very good learning experience. We got to know people that shared their experiences with us. We got to know other parts of Brazil too, and this helped a lot. This helped us better understand what we were doing there. After those almost four years of movement, I matured a lot; I didn't know what kind of reality I was living. I learned that it is our struggle; that we have to fight for the right to have our own house, a place to call home. If we don't try, we won't get there. If this ship sinks, I want to sink with it, fight until the end. (Male, 33 years old, translated from Portuguese by the authors and G. Moellwald)

It is in the relationships among subjects that they are affected, changed and established as beings of and within a certain social and cultural group: "After those almost four years of movement, I matured a lot; I didn't know what kind of reality I was living. I learned that it is our struggle; that we have to fight for the right of having our own house, a place to call home". The different backgrounds of people, different prior experiences, their personal values and individualities make the *Occupation* a large school of human coexistence. Everyone must reorganize on a personal and social level as a resident of the Occupation and member of MNLM.

Cultural belonging presupposes sharing ideas, values, attitudes, practices, and decisions. In this sense, language has a central role in the communication between individuals and in the establishment of collective meanings that constitute a certain world vision, fundamental for the establishment of common goals and the subjects' commitment to the struggle. It is in the *praxis*, understood as the reflection and action of people upon the world to change it and the condition for overcoming oppressive relations, that the human being becomes aware of him/herself and the world. It is in the *praxis* that the subject signifies his/her experience and communicates as an expression of his/her thought-language. In other words:

> The word, as basis for comprehension, calls for change and becomes inseparable from the need for action: it thus becomes word-action, to use Paulo Freire's neologism. From the moment someone understands and becomes aware of one's role in the world, change becomes inevitable and therefore generates an action to achieve such goal. (Rossato, 2008, p. 331, translated from Portuguese by the authors and G. Moellwald)

Therefore, we believe that dialogue, the interexchange of experience through language, can propitiate transformative actions, both in the individual and in society. Dialogue is, thus, an aggregating movement, a wise movement that preserves its strengths while also producing new strengths capable of confronting the discourses that immobilize and hinder further action.

> What we want is for people to continue thinking about the world, even if they eventually leave the movement when they find a place to live, when they find a job. You can't think that because you solved your problem you don't need to be involved in the struggle. I cannot choose not to change the world, because we are always taking part in it, like it or not, so I can at least think about what kind of change I want to bring to the world. (Male, 26 years old, translated from Portuguese by the authors and G. Moellwald)

The narrative above is a demonstration of the subject's acknowledgement of being historically conditioned, but not determined, as when he affirms that: "I cannot choose not to change the world, because we are always taking part in it". Subjects overcome the "limit-situations" that imprison them in an apparently immutable reality when they see their experience from afar: "I can at least think of what kind of change I want to bring to the world". Thus the concrete historical dimensions that challenge subjects to try to overcome and build a "viable unprecedented" reality are revealed, conceived as a dream that continuously gains potential of being fulfilled. At the same time, by evoking one's words, the subject is empowered, increasingly envisioning oneself as a protagonist of his own history (Freire, 1987).

The eviction that the group had previously experienced had been documented in the publication *Moradia é Central* (Kohara, Uemura, & Ferro, 2012, p. 46): "in 2006, 21 families associated to MNLM occupied a building downtown and were evicted in 2007 in a major operation with over 300 police officers that stopped the city center". A member reports on the moment of eviction:

> When the police arrived to remove us from the Mauá building, you should have seen the number of cops. The riot police even came with the caverão (armored vehicle). The judicial officer was really nice, didn't want violence, but we could not just leave without putting up a resistance. They closed the streets giving access to the building, which completely shut down the downtown. It was madness, it seemed like a war operation. Imagine us there, a bunch of families, children, what danger could we offer? We began singing our songs of resistance and command words, even to reduce the tension, because people were afraid, people with children. We recorded everything from the window, we thought they would invade. But they didn't. After a lot of talking, we were able to negotiate the space we occupy today with a city representative. So we left there singing peacefully and a city truck brought us here. (Male, 36 years old, translated from Portuguese by the authors and G. Moellwald)

We see this sharing of memories as a process of constitution of meanings in which a place and an active role is granted to the narrator and the listener respectively. The subjects narrate their struggle as protagonists of their stories instead of passive spectators of norms prescribed to them: "we could not just leave without putting up a resistance". The story of conflict with the police narrated by the subject sheds light on the strategies of resistance created within MNLM, and how these strategies enabled the group to negotiate with a public authority and conquer a new living space, even if only temporarily: "we were able to negotiate with a city representative the space we occupy today". Thus, positions of other subjects were engendered in the narratives, affirming their own voices as protagonists of the struggle for a fairer society.

Final Considerations: The Broader Sense of Popular Education

In the development of the documentary with the residents of the November 20 Occupation, we, researchers, learned that housing is a right on the basis of which people organize their lives. Housing also means having access to education, health, recreation, and income. We experienced the permanent tensions of power relations that produce, along with symbolic goods, social materiality. That is, a game of forces in which different perspectives of the city come to play, in which other ways of urban life are possible.

We aimed, in the production of the documentary as well as in this text, to reaffirm the commitment of researchers to social movements and their struggles. The goal of building a democratic society demands that we meet the interests and needs of different groups, especially those historically, socially, politically, and economically excluded from society, and that we acknowledge the legitimacy of their cultural processes. Thus, we sought to contribute to the process of affirmation of excluded voices, in this case the struggle, the fight for a right, the fight for social justice. Echoing the voice of the protagonists of the Struggle for Housing, we sought to emphasize the group's ideas and their experience in a work developed *with the other* and not *for the other*, following the principles of Popular Education.

To conclude, we can affirm that, in the struggle, apprehending and questioning reality means transcending it, even if the subject's awareness is not the only all-powerful instance that invents his/her social reality (Freire & Macedo, 1990). The participants, by narrating their experiences and the meanings behind the Occupation, reaffirmed and strengthened themselves, as well as their collective struggle. In this context, empowerment is the result of a social *praxis*, or, in other words, of the problematization and critical reflection of people that place them in a position to change the reality oppressing them.

The theoretical perspective of Popular Education used here does not refer only to the formal instances of education, but to processes of development, as described by Freire, "of human beings departing from who they are to who they want to be" (Romão, 2008, p. 150). In this context educating oneself is a much broader experience, characterized as a political act of living in the human collective. The National Movement of Struggle for Housing (MNLM), materialized in the November 20 Occupation, can be characterized as a significant educational and pedagogical experience toward a different, novel way of living.

References

Baquero, R. V. A. (2012). Empoderamento: Instrumento de emancipação social? Uma discussão conceitual. *Revista Debates: Revista de Ciências Sociais*, 6(1), 173–187. Retrieved from <http://seer.ufrgs.br/debates/article/view/26722> [date of access: 27/05/16].

Brandão, C. R. (2006). A pesquisa participante e a participação da pesquisa. In C. R. Brandão & D. R. Streck (Eds), *Pesquisa participante: A partilha do saber* (pp. 21–54). Aparecida, SP: Ideias & Letras.

Brandão, C. R., & Assumpção, R. (2009). *Cultura rebelde: Escritos sobre a educação popular ontem e agora*. São Paulo, SP: Editora e Livraria Instituto Paulo Freire.

Brunetto, G., & Souza, M. (Directors). (2012). *A copa dos 20 de novembro* [Video file, 23:50 min]. Retrieved from <https://www.youtube.com/watch?v=2JsRIBNZgMc> [date of access: 27/05/16].

Buonfiglio, L. V. (2007). *O resgate do centro de Porto Alegre: A luta dos sem-teto pelo direito à moradia.* (Master's dissertation, Universidade de Brasília). Retrieved from <http://repositorio.unb.br/handle/10482/2926>.

Curi, M. (2013). A disputa pelo legado em megaeventos esportivos no Brasil. *Horizontes Antropológicos*, 19(40), 65–88. <doi:10.1590/S0104-71832013000200003>.

Freire, P. (1981). *Ação cultural para a liberdade* (5th ed.). Rio de Janeiro: Paz e Terra.

Freire, P. (1983). *Educação como prática da liberdade* (6th ed.). Rio de Janeiro: Paz e Terra.

Freire, P. (1986). *A importância do ato de ler: Em três artigos que se completam* (16th ed.). São Paulo: Cortez.

Freire, P. (1987). *Pedagogia do oprimido* (17th ed.) Rio de Janeiro: Paz e Terra.

Freire, P. (1992). *Pedagogia da esperança: Um encontro com a pedagogia do oprimido* (8th ed). Rio de Janeiro: Paz e Terra.

Freire, P., & Macedo, D. (1990). *Alfabetização: Leitura do mundo, leitura da palavra* (3rd ed.). Rio de Janeiro: Paz e Terra.

Freire, P., & Shor, I. (1986). *Medo e ousadia: O cotidiano do professor* (5th ed.). Rio de Janeiro: Paz e Terra.

Gohn, M. G. (1991). *Movimentos sociais e lutas pela moradia*. São Paulo: Edições Loyola.

Instituto de Pesquisa Econômica Aplicada – IPEA. (n.d.). *Estado das cidades do mundo 2010/2011: Unindo o urbano dividido*. United Nations Human Settlements Programme. Retrieved from <http://www.ipea.gov.br/agencia/images/stories/ PDFs/100408_cidadesdomundo_portugues.pdf> [date of access: 27/05/16].

Kohara, L., Uemura, M. M., & Ferro, M. C. T. (Eds) (2012). *Moradia é central: Lutas, desafios e estratégias*. Centro Gaspar Garcia de Direitos Humanos. Retrieved from <http://www.polis.org.br/uploads/1512/1512.pdf> [date of access: 27/05/16]

Kontopodis, M. Magalhães, M. C. & Coracini, M. J. (this volume). Fifty years of critical research in Brazil: An introduction. In: M. Kontopodis, M. C. Magalhães, & M. J. Coracini (Eds), *Facing Poverty and Marginalization: Fifty Years of Critical Research in Brazil*. Oxford: Peter Lang.

McDonogh, G. (2002). Discourse of the city: Policy and response in post-transitional Barcelona. In S. M. Low (Ed.), *Theorizing the city* (pp. 342–376). New Brunswick, NJ and London: Rutgers University Press.

Nello, O. (1997). The Olympic Games as a tool for urban renewal: the experience of Barcelona '92 Olympic Village. In M. de Moragas, M. Linés, & B. Kidd (Eds), *Olympic villages: A hundred years of urban planning and shared experiences – International Symposium on Olympic Villages* (pp. 91–96). Lausanne: International Olympic Committee.

Paludo, C. (2001). *Educação Popular em busca de alternativas: Uma leitura desde o campo democrático popular*. Porto Alegre: Tomo Editorial e Camp.

Perlman, J. (2010). *Favela: Four decades of living on the edge in Rio de Janeiro*. Oxford: Oxford University Press.

Ribeiro, L. C. (2014). Por uma análise social e política dos megaeventos esportivos no Brasil. *Ciência e Cultura*, 66(2), 27–30. Retrieved from <http://cienciaecultura. bvs.br/pdf/cic/v66n2/v66n2a12.pdf> [date of access: 27/05/16].

Romão, J. E. (2008). Educação. In D. R. Streck, E. Redin, & J. J. Zitkoski (Eds), *Dicionário Paulo Freire* (pp. 150–152). Belo Horizonte: Autêntica.

Rossato, R. (2008). Práxis. In D. R. Streck, E. Redin, & J. J. Zitkoski (Eds), *Dicionário Paulo Freire* (pp. 331–333). Belo Horizonte: Autêntica.

Secretaria Geral da Presidência da República (2014). *Desapropriações e deslocamentos involuntários na Copa FIFA 2014*. Retrieved from <http://secretariageral.gov.br/ noticias/2014/julho/gilberto-carvalho-faz-coletiva-sobre-democracia-e-grandes- eventos/copa_2014_desapropriacoes-final-1.pdf> [date of access: 27/05/16].

Smith, N. (1996). *The new urban frontier: Gentrification and revanchist city*. New York and London: Routledge.

ISABELA CAMINI & MICHALIS KONTOPODIS

3.   Educating in Itinerancy: Countryside Life and Novel Forms of Schooling

Partially translated from Portuguese by Ana Schäffer

Introduction

The purpose of this chapter is to explore the access to education for the Landless Rural Workers who have been itinerants due to the struggle for agrarian reform in Brazil – a struggle that began in the early 1980s. The Landless Rural Worker's Movement in Brazil (Movimento dos Trabalhadores Rurais Sem Terra, MST or MTST) is considered the major counter-hegemonic movement of Brazil and one of the most important radical social movements of Latin America, with an estimated 1.5 million landless members of all possible ages and ethnic-racial groups organized all over Brazil (cf. Karriem, 2009, Kontopodis, 2013).

The Landless Workers – who mainly came from urbanized populations who had not survived well in urban spaces or who had formerly been very low-paid agribusiness workers without owning any land (therefore "landless"), began occupying land that was owned by colonial landlords but was not used around 1984 –the movement was founded in that year during the 1st Meeting of the Landless Rural Workers in Cascavel, Paraná). Marking a great rupture with the colonial legacy of land ownership in Brazil, all occupied land has been owned, administered and cultivated collectively and there has been no private ownership (therefore the rural workers still call themselves Landless). The main quest of the Landless Movement was the "Agrarian Reform" i.e. the re-distribution of land all over Brazil – a quest that remains until today.

Establishing such a radical social movement, has not obviously been straightforward; In 2009, the special issue of the Landless Workers' own newspaper commemorating the 25th anniversary of the Landless Movement, presented a detailed historical narrative – to mention only three major events: 19 Landless Workers were gunned down dead and another 69 wounded by police while they were blocking a state road in Pará on April 17, 1996 (Eldorado dos Carajás massacre). Another 13,000 Landless Workers marched from Goiânia to Brasilia (more than 200 kilometers) in 2005 (Jornal dos Trabalhadores Rurais Sem Terra, 2009). As Hannah Wittman writes, continuous occupations, negotiations, displacements, encampments, settlements, resettlements, and a series of demonstrations and violent confrontations with police marked slowly the transitions from individuals to imagined communities, from imagined communities to collectivities, and from collectivities to place-based communities (Wittman, 2005).

The Landless Workers introduced a significant distinction between two opposed forms of agricultural production: *agribusiness* and *agroecology*. *Agribusiness* has had a long history of exploitation of the local populations in Brazil that can be traced back to colonial times. In the context of *agribusiness* local populations often had not had access to any proper food at all, for the shake of export-oriented production. On the contrary, *agroecology* had been based on a quite simple idea: the modern family (not a huge "medieval family" or any other group constellation) produces the food that it needs to survive: rice, beans, chicken, fruit – which is the primary production. At another place (either individually or collectively) coffee, allspice, or other products are cultivated for sale. This secondary production aims to ensure access to products that are bought such as freezers, pumps, clothes, electricity, construction materials, and whatever else the Landless Workers need but do not produce on their own.

In this frame, the Landless Workers faced the following necessity: scientific research and knowledge as well as educational practices in agronomy had been developed previously to the Landless Movement in order to support and improve large-scale agribusiness. Small-scale agroecology demanded very different knowledge, technologies and skills – that still needed to be developed by the Landless Workers – here both referring to children and adults. This yet-to-be-developed knowledge involved geology, agrophysics and agrochemistry as well as ecology as to design small-scale agriculture in ecological-friendly and effective ways. However it also involved geography and population statistics ("how many are we, where?"), economics ("how to sell fruits and buy water pumps?") and political history and economy ("why is land owned by very few big landlords and how can this be changed?") (cf. Bonamigo, 2007; Kontopodis, 2012).

Soon alphabetization became a priority for the Landless Workers' Movement. Access to education and participation in knowledge production became a political claim that was as important as the claim for land (Camini, 2008). The Movement realized quickly that for its radical politics to be further developed new schools needed then to be established – not only new curricula, but new schools, which meant differently educated teachers, with broader socio-political aspirations who would be part of the movement and not external to it and be able to organize educational activities that would lead to creating new bodies of knowledge. Furthermore, the Landless Workers' Movement based its actions on the idea of locating a school where the Landless Workers live – and not far away in nearby towns or cities (Camini, 2008).

Our analysis below, explores the first steps of this undertaking i.e. the practice of setting up a school as soon as an encampment took place, in the first steps of the movement. We will focus primarily on three Brazilian states: Para, Parana and Rio Grande do Sul, where in view of the continuity of the settlements, significant struggles for establishment of schools in encampments took place. The chapter discusses a few major developments in the field, which took place in parallel in the 1990s: the formalization of the Itinerant School (IS), the creation of hundreds of settlement schools, and the commencement of the first academic debates on "countryside education".

Schooling in the Encampment

The history of the education and schooling of the Landless Rural Workers' Movement dates back to the earliest encampments in the struggle for land in the historical occupations of the unproductive latifúndios, i.e. large landholdings (of about 10,000 hectares in average) Annoni Farm in 1985,

Giacomet Farm in 1996 and Macaxeira Farm in Eldorado dos Carajas in 1996. Despite the problems with the school infrastructure and the content of the curriculum, creating schools in those encampments was one of the first steps taken into creating a community life:

> The first building is ready: it's a *school*. A large, long and ventilated rancho with cover and internal walls – from a class to another – covered with babassu straw. Joaquim tells me quite simply, 'most people I know went to cities in searching of schooling for their children or medical treatment. In the city, sometimes they find schools for their children, but they don't find employment for the adults. In the rural areas, there are jobs for adults, but there is no school for children. For this reason, the school is as important as the road for us to arrive in Parauapebas or bank financing. We want our children to learn more than we did. They must not grow up like wild animals of the jungle. The school, in a certain way, is the soul of the settlement. So, I ask: What about the educational supplies? We rely on the government for these. But the spelling-books belong to us. We don't want the government to poison our kids' minds. There are other places around here, which are populated and exist for over ten years, but there is not even a school there. Here, the school building was the first step we took. (Tierra, 1996, p. 9)

Similarly, during the occupation process of the Giacomet Farm, in Parana state, one of the first initiatives was to organize the school; it was taken for granted that this was necessary from the beginning of the encampment. According to Monteiro,

> It didn't take that much time until the first school was negotiated [...] As soon as the families arrived at the encampment headquarter, they organized a negotiation team that would be in charge of negotiating the creation of a school at the encampment with the relevant public authorities. (Monteiro, 2003, p. 45)

The location and the infrastructure of the school were not of primary importance. Nevertheless, the right to have a school should have been assured. Our research team found a record on the local registers of a shed in the farm headquarters that was rebuilt by the collective work of those encamped into a school. Thus, the space that had previously been used for keeping machines and agricultural tools was now serving as a classroom. This initiative, including the incorporation of secondary school level in addition to the already existent elementary level, assured the right to schooling for the children of the encamped, and when later they moved to another settlement, they attended the "State School Iraci Salete Strozak", at the settlement Marcos Freire, in the city of Rio Bonito do Iguaçu, Parana. Currently, that school has 36 teachers and 520 students who are children of the families that live in the surrounding settlements. Recently, the settled communities have celebrated this accomplishment, as it has assured them the right to study in a school, which was organized by the peasants (rural workers) without depending on a school bus as to study in the city, far removed from the context of their everyday lives.

At the encampment of Annoni Farm (1986), the initiative to organize the school, and to pursue its legalization, also assured the schooling of hundreds of countryside children. Some years later, when the area was transformed into an officially recognized settlement, the itinerant school automatically became the "settlement school". As the families were organized and the number of children of school age was increasing, the demand forced the creation of five more public, state and local schools in the region, which have achieved quite high results in official evaluations and statistics on countryside schools (Camini, 2009b).

Itinerant School and Countryside Education

When analysing the history of the Landless Rural Workers' Movement, it becomes evident that 1995 was a decisive year for the landless children in Rio Grande do Sul. Many children lived in the encampments, mostly attending schools not recognized by the state. The children then *got on the scene* and began by organizing themselves and holding meetings. The first one in 1994, and the second, in 1995 were called "Infanto-juvenil Congress" (Childrens' & Young Peoples' Congress), and later, "Encontro dos Sem Terrinha" (Meeting of Landless Children).

In October 1995, at the second meeting, which took place in Porto Alegre, the children studied the 1990's Child and Adolescent Statute, among other activities. This study was important for the children to understand that education – one of the basic rights assured by Brazilian Federal

Constitution – was being curtailed because they were encamped with their parents in the struggle for Agrarian Reform. According to own children's reports, the decision was to "fight for their school's legalization so they could be accredited for completing the academic year". Many of them attended school at the encampment, and whilst it had brought them remarkable learning, it was not recognized by the government. Therefore, they would not be able to enter the next grade.

Once mobilized, the children took their idea to Iara Silvia Wortmann, Secretary of Education, who accepted the challenge and immediately initiated the development of a pedagogical proposal which was developed on the basis of an agreement with the Education Sector of the South of Brazil Landless Workers' Movement and the members of the Education Secretariat. The result was the adoption of the so-called "Itinerant School" legislation on 19 November 1996. From this date on, and throughout 1997, the proposal was implemented, studied, and discussed in two encampments: Palmeirão, in the city of Julio de Castilhos, and Santo Antonio, in Santo Antonio das Missões, where there were most families together, and the schools were working. It is important to mention that the families working in favor of planning and organizing the school – before the legalization of the referred encampments – joined together and forced the elaboration of the Itinerant School proposal, which was then unanimously approved by the State Council of Education.

It is pertinent to recall that at the time, particularly at the beginning of 1998, a debate had begun on *countryside education*, resulting in the State Meeting for a Basic Countryside Education, organized in partnership with the Federal University of Rio Grande do Sul (UFRGS), the Center of Teachers of the State of Rio Grande do Sul, the Union of Workers in Education, the Landless Workers Movement, and the Land Pastoral Committee of Rio Grande do Sul. The event took place in Porto Alegre, State of Rio Grande do Sul, at the Federal University of Rio Grande do Sul, on 26–29 May, with representatives from these organizations (Foerste & Kontopodis, 2012).

At that time, those organizations were questioning the schooling provided by the typical rural schools in the Brazilian countryside and the curriculum they followed (which was same to the one addressed to urban populations). They therefore had the disposition to take a step forward with regard to thinking about other schooling types such as the itinerant one, making the countryside people the protagonists of their own education.

Meetings took place in at least 20 states of Brazil in order to prepare the National Conference for Basic Countryside Education, which was held in Luziania (Goias State), on 27–31 July 1998. The partner organizations were the National Conference of Brazilian Bishops, the Rural Landless Workers' Movement, the United Nations Educational, Scientific and Cultural organization (UNESCO), the United Nations for Children's Fund (UNICEF), and the National University of Brasilia, with around one thousand people participating including not only educators but also other participants such as children, parents, policy-makers and researchers. The Itinerant School of the Landless Rural Workers' Movement became therefore a driving force of the broader Countryside Education movement.

Countryside education (educação do campo) – as opposed to *rural* education (educação rural) – is a broader term that comprises and respects the heterogeneity of schools and educational institutions, that are organized in very different ways in the Brazilian countryside with an emphasis on social justice, which is not often ensured through large scale agribusiness: Federal Agrotechnical Schools, Municipal School of Agroecological Education, Centers of Agroecological Education, centrally or locally administered Schools of Pedagogy of Alternation ("Escolas Familias"), Communitarian Rural Schools, Indigenous Schools, Quilombolas (former black slaves) Schools, Pomeran Schools, Schools of Fishermen, various schools for people who work with rubber ("seringueiros"), in extraction or in the cacao plantations, Integrated State Centers of Countryside Education, Schools of the Settlements of Landless Rural Workers (Iniciativa da Carta da Terra Brasil, 2000).

Fighting for Legal Recognition

From 1996 to 2002, the Landless Rural Workers' Movement came under strong pressure and was attacked by the ruling class and the representatives of local governments (Camini, 2009a). Nevertheless the attacks and pressures on the Movement did not prevent mobilizations in several states in order to obtain legal recognition of the schooling of hundreds of students studying in schools organized in encampments. Several publications around that time provided strong statements in support of such legal recognition (Kolling, Néry & Molina, 1999; Secretaria de Estado da Educação, 2002).

The Landless Rural Workers' Movement of the State of Parana was the first to make the political decision to negotiate the legalization of the students' schooling from non-yet-recognized encampment schools. A team of local teachers and researchers studied a variety of teaching and training practices in the encampments and drafted the Pedagogical Proposal for the Itinerant School, which was approved by the State Council of Education of Parana on 8 December 2003. Initially, this referred to the schools at encampments, but as soon as the families moved from encampments to permanent settlements in areas formally released for the Landless Workers to live and cultivate land, the schools moved to the settlements as well (which is entailed in the meaning of the word "itinerant"). At the time this chapter is written, there are 12 itinerant schools with 350 educators who have been teaching around 800 students in elementary and secondary education in the State of Parana.

Similar developments took place in the State of Santa Catarina in Rio Grande do Sul, where, the State Councils of Education also approved the Itinerant School Proposal on 21 September 2004 and then in the State of Goias, the State of Alagoas, etc. Although the figures constantly change as the Agrarian Reform may move forward or lose ground depending on the broader political situation in Brazil, the Landless Rural Workers' Movement currently boasts 37 schools with about 400 teachers, in six states of Brazil, serving around 4,000 students. These students would have otherwise, either not attended any school at all, or upon finishing non-recognized, locally organized schools been denied recognition and access to further education or to the local and national job market (Camini, 2001).

Outlook: Current Issues and Challenges

We agree with the educator, poet and Cuban political leader, José Martí, when referring to the importance of peasants having a school nearby and learning through curricula that are connected to their every day realities.

For Martí as for the Landless Workers, it is unacceptable that the people of the countryside have to move away from the social practices that involve them, in order to attend school:

> The peasant cannot leave his job to walk several miles to see incomprehensible geometric figures, and learn the capes and rivers of the African peninsulas, and get stuffed full of empty educational terms. The peasants' children can't get away entire leagues, day after day, from their parents' ranch in order to learn Latin declinations and abbreviated divisions. And he goes on, referring to that time: the itinerant school can solve the peasant's ignorance. In the countryside as in cities, it is urgent to replace the indirect and sterile knowledge of books with the direct and fertile knowledge of nature. (Martí, 1995, pp. 44–46)

We see that, although he had lived in a different historical and social context, Martí's reflections on the school of the peasants take into account the realities of the Brazilian Landless Workers. He emphasizes the need to create itinerant schools that provide the opportunity for people to study and work at the same time. Decisive about these schools' function, is also the content that should be studied in these schools and be interesting, accessible and relevant for the countryside children. Aware of the realities of Cuban peasants and what they would probably learn in the schools of the city, the Cuban poet is emphatic when referring to the content taught by these schools. For what and for whom is the content taken from sterile textbooks?

These same questions should have been asked many times by the Landless Rural Workers' teachers and educators. All educators of the countryside need to ask themselves: why is certain content, aged by the time, out of date, disconnected from the students' lives, and called "minimum curriculum", imposed by the school system? Where do textbooks come from and who is authoring them and placing them in our libraries without any guidance on how to use them? With regard to the knowledge that the peasants need in the countryside school, Miguel Gonzalez Arroyo points out,

> We need to work with live knowledge! [...] one that gives answers, that interprets the questions coming from the past and the present [...] Why do the big questions that face the world of the countryside today have no place in the curricula of schools of the countryside? Why is the knowledge of the countryside people never considered "knowledge"? (Arroyo, 2005, p. 7)

The itinerant school curriculum indeed reflects the "lessons" being "taught" outside the classroom, while the student-teacher relationship is of central importance. This is only possible because the school is physically and pedagogically immersed in the countryside environment and soaked in the social atmosphere of the struggle for Agrarian Reform in Brazil. Therefore, its organization and planning frequently results from the concrete struggles and the changing social circumstances in which it is embedded (Hammel & Andretta, 2007). Yet, systematization and pedagogical reflection on the social practices that arise in schools takes place, as well.

Theoretical work by Anton Semjonovitsj Makarenko and Paulo Freire inspired in this context a different pedagogics: beginning from the everyday lives of the landless people and what they already knew in order to teach them something abstracter – even if it was chemistry or physics became a common teaching strategy in the context of the Landless Movement schools (cf. Foerste & Kontopodis, 2012). In other words, the itinerant school became a school which, to some extent, has been able to interweave with the countryside people's lives, respecting their social circumstances, welcoming their feelings of pain, anger or joy. Furthermore, learning was thus organized as a participatory collaborative activity of creating knowledge that had still not been available and was needed as to develop small-scale sustainable agro-ecological production (cf. Kontopodis, 2012).

For the first time in the history of Brazil countryside populations demanded in that context a differentiated education for them – a school that would appeal to their various local needs, customs, languages, and histories and at the same time enable them to pursue further education in central universities, and enjoy social mobility later on. Itinerant schools are proclaimed to be a *new* form of schooling, operating in the periphery of academic and political debates for *new* educational conceptions and practices. The itinerant school questions the *old* school – one that provides a decontextualized curriculum, divorced from students' lives, physically stagnated, and pedagogically choked. Those schools, divorced from their students' lives, are the reason why the students have a strong desire to escape their walls (Foerste, Foerste-Schütz & Duarte-Schneider, 2008).

The *countryside* – the place of life and work of peasants, requires indeed *another* kind of school, different in all aspects from the usual school currently in function in the countryside and in the city. What is more: *countryside education* is rising with another vision – to give time and voice to the countryside populations so they can build *different* and *new* schools that give priority to all various dimensions of human formation (formação/ Bildung) – including political economy and (colonial) history (Luciano, 2008). That much work yet remains in this area is both exciting and a challenge.

References

Arroyo, M. G. (2005). Que educação básica para os povos do campo? *Seminário Nacional "Educação básica nas áreas de Reforma Agrária do MST"*, 12–16 September 2005. Luziânia.

Bonamigo, C. A. (2007). *Pedagogias que brotam da terra: Um estudo sobre práticas educativas do campo*. (PhD Dissertation). Porto Alegre: Programa de Pós-Graduação em Educação, Faculdade de Educação, Universidade Federal do Rio Grande do Sul.

Camini, I. (2001) (Ed.). *Escola itinerante: Uma prática pedagógica em acampamentos*. São Paulo: Setor de Educação do MST.

Camini, I. (2008) O significado da escola itinerante para o MST. *DESAFIOS – Cadernos da Comissão de Educação, Cultura, Desporto, Ciência e Tecnologia da Assembléia Legislativa do Rio Grande do Sul*, 2(3), 55–68.

Camini, I. (2009a). Escola itinerante dos acampamentos do MST: Um contraponto à escola capitalista? *Cadernos da Escola Itinerante – MST*, 2(3), 121–139.

Camini, I. (2009b). *Escola itinerante: Na fronteira de uma nova escola*. São Paulo: Expressão Popular.

Foerste, E., Foerste-Schütz, M. G., & Duarte-Schneider, L. M. (Eds). (2008). *Projeto político-pedagógico da educação do campo/Por uma educação do campo vol. 6*. Vitória: PRONERA na Região Sudeste.

Foerste, E., & Kontopodis, M. (2012). Die Pädagogik der Erde (Pedagogia da Terra) als Herausforderung für die Erziehungswissenschaften: Eine Bewertung der Partnerschaft zwischen der Bewegung der Landlosen („Movimento Sem Terra") und der Bundesuniversität Espírito Santo in Brasilien. *Journal für tätigkeitstheoretische Forschung in Deutschland*, 9, 87–106, Open Access/Online: <http:// www.ich-sciences.de/pages/posts/heft-9-85.php> (date of access: 6/06/2016).

Hammel, A. C., Silva, N. J. C., & Andretta, R. (2007) (Eds). *Escola em movimento*. Rio Bonito do Iguaçu: Colégio Estadual Iraci Salete Strozak.

Iniciativa da Carta da Terra Brasil. (2000). *Carta da Terra*. Brazil: <http://www. cartadaterrabrasil.com.br/prt/index.html> (date of access: 3/06/2016).

Jornal dos Trabalhadores Rurais Sem Terra. (2009). 25 anos de lutas a conquistas. *Jornal dos Trabalhadores Rurais Sem Terra/Edição Especial: MST 25 Anos 1984–2009*, pp. 6–11.

Karriem, A. (2009). The rise and transformation of the Brazilian landless movement into a counter-hegemonic political actor: A Gramscian analysis. *Geoforum*, 40(3), 316–325.

Kolling, E. J, Néry, I. J., & Molina, M. C. (Eds) (1999). *Por uma educação básica do campo*. Brasília: Articulação Nacional Por Uma Educação Básica do Campo.

Kontopodis, M. (2012). *Neoliberalism, pedagogy and human development: Exploring time, mediation and collectivity in contemporary schools*. London and New York: Routledge/Taylor & Francis.

Kontopodis, M. (2013). Trinta anos de construção identitária Sem Terra no Espírito Santo: Explorando um projeto político-pedagógico de vanguarda contra o neo-liberalismo. *Perspectiva*, 31(3), 919–938.

Luciano, C. L. P. (2008). *Escola Itinerante: Uma análise das práticas educativas do MST no contexto da democracia liberal*. Santa Cruz do Sul: EDUNISC.

Martí, J. (1995). *Vida e obra*. São Paulo: Peres.

Monteiro, G. (2003). Colégio Iraci Salete Stronzake: Conquistando o latifúndio do saber. Instituto de Educação José de Castro – Alternativas de escolarização dos adolescentes em assentamentos e acampamentos do MST. *Cadernos do ITERRA* 8, 41–60.

Secretaria de Estado da Educação (2002). *II conferência estadual por uma educação básica do campo*. Porto Alegre: Secretaria de Estado da Educação.

Tierra, P. (1996). Eldorado: Notícia dos sobreviventes: Para Isabel que tece os cordões da resistência. *Teoria e Debate*, 32, 4–13.

Wittman, H. (2005). Agrarian reform and the production of locality: resettlement and community building in Mato Grosso, Brazil. *Revista Nera*, 8(7), 94–111.

4. Indigenous Children and Identity Politics: Numeracy Practices among the Kaiabi from Xingu, Mato Grosso

Introduction

Historically, indigenous education in Brazil was characterized by two prevailing "total immersion" agendas. According to the one, indigenous children were taken away from their communities in order to receive a monolingual education in Portuguese, following an official school curriculum. According to the other agenda, however, bilingual education was advocated, although the indigenous language actually had a subordinate role, being a medium of instruction in elementary school until the necessary proficiency in Portuguese was attained. In opposition to such models, and in the quest for indigenous schooling aimed at linguistic preservation and the cultural maintenance of indigenous peoples (Cavalcanti & Maher, 1993), a third agenda has established itself recognizing the need for intercultural and multilingual indigenous schooling.

Since the 1988 constitution came into force, recognizing the 180 indigenous languages spoken in Brazil, a process for developing indigenous schools began to address the cultural specificities of each group and to contribute to the process of the acquisition of autonomy by indigenous communities. The combination of this concern with the acquisition of autonomy with the obvious socio-cultural and linguistic diversity of indigenous groups in Brazil, drew attention to the need for indigenous teachers and led to the development of educational programs to train these teachers. These programs began in the 1980s through projects developed by non-governmental organizations. These projects were developed with the participation of university consultants from different fields such as anthropology, linguistics, and education. In the mid-1990s, further programs had been set up by state education bureaus and universities.

The attempt to create and establish multilingual and intercultural indigenous schools resulted in discussions about the curriculum (Ministério da Educação, 1998) and an increase in the development of bilingual materials by indigenous teachers during their training. In this context, the purpose of this chapter is to discuss questions about identity processes that arise from the production of materials written by indigenous teachers in indigenous languages. The discussion is based on ethnographic research carried out in the multilingual context of Xingu Indigenous Park. The research continued to study indigenous teachers' education over five years. Xingu Indigenous Park is located in the center of Brazil, in the State of Mato Grosso, and has an area of 6,532,158 acres. This Indian Reserve is crossed by the Xingu River and divided into two regions called Lower Xingu (in the North) and Upper Xingu (in the South). Fifteen ethnic groups currently live there: Kuikuro, Kalapalo, Matipu, Nahukuá, Mehinaku, Waurá, Aweti, Kamaiurá, Trumai, Ikpeng, Yawalapiti, Suya, Kaiabi, Yudjá,), and Kayapo.

Our so-called "Indigenous Teacher Education Project" was funded and supported by the NGO Instituto Socioambiental in Brazil and saw the participation of 55 teachers from all 15 ethnics groups in the Xingu Park. Courses took place twice a year, lasting one month at a time, for 6 years. The research data is from my field notes, taken at the time when I was giving the courses and visiting the schools and the communities, as well as from interviews with indigenous teachers.

During the courses, indigenous teachers made a math book to be used for teaching mathematics in their schools as part of a collaborative project. When I proposed this task, I asked them whether they wanted to make one book for all indigenous groups in Portuguese, or if each ethnic group would prefer to have their own book, written in their own indigenous language. Faced with this question, they chose to write it in their indigenous languages; they wanted to have their own book. Whilst producing the book, the Kaiabi teachers initially faced a problem writing a math book in their indigenous language: They had problems with the numbers, because the Kaiabi language only has words for numbers up to five. Nevertheless, they wanted a Kaiabi math book.

It is important to point out that producing written material in indigenous languages actualized a certain type of identity politics, in which the book written in a native language became a marker of indigenous identity. Arising from this, one question of inquiry was: How do identity issues link to indigenous teachers' education? "Indigenous identity" is approached here from a discursive perspective. Identity is constructed *in* and *through* language – not in a fixed or essentialist sense, but in constant motion. Identity processes are always built in relation to and dependent upon the nature of social relations that are established over time (cf. Kontopodis & Matera, 2010). The theoretical basis of this study is discourse analysis (Fairclough, 1999; Balloco, 2006), applied linguistics (Maher, 1996, 2010), cultural studies (Hall, 1997, Woodward, 1997) and post-colonial studies (Bhabha, 1994).

I centered the discussion about identity issues on Kaiabi teachers' discourse about the numerical terms in their indigenous language, as presented below. The chapter explores the Kaiabi cultural meaning of "number" within their community practices as well as arising from the contact with non-indigenous society. It highlights the symbolic and political facets of the expansion of numerical terminology in indigenous language by teachers, elders, and community leaders in their attempt to produce a Kaiabi math book.

The Kaiabi at Xingu Indigenous Park

> "Do you know that berry called "kaja"?" The kaja was on the floor, and my grandmother said: "Come toucan; eat the berry." The saint spoke, "Come toucan and eat", and the toucan came and ate the fruit. We are born of this kaja's seed [...] Then, the white man came and began to speak kaja, kaja, kaja, kaja, kaia kaia, kaia ... kaiabi.
> — IPEPORI KAIABI, August, 1998[1]

[1] All extracts are translated from Portuguese and/or the various local languages by the author.

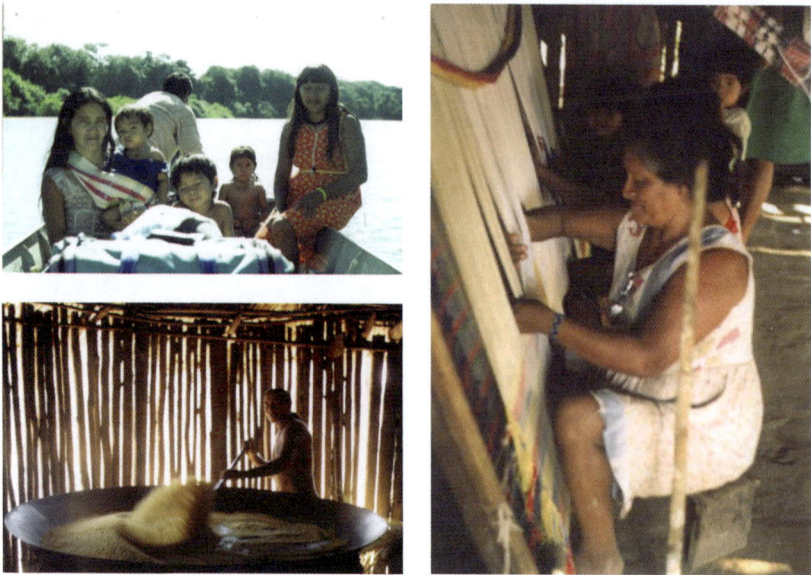

Fig. 1. Kaiabi people (photographed by the author)

Ipepori Kaiabi (known as Prepori) told the story above. He was an important Kaiabi *paje* (shaman), who died in April, 2000. He played an important role, along with Claudio Villas Boas, in the displacement of the Kaiabi from their original territory to Xingu Indigenous Park. This story invokes issues concerning the names assigned to the indigenous groups in Brazil. Their various names are generally names given from the outside, either by non-indigenous groups who came in contact with the indigenous people, or through contact with other indigenous groups. Although many groups are known by names such as Kaiabi, Karaja, Zoro, and Suruí, amongst others, these people do not call themselves by these names. For example, the Surui people said that this name was given to them by anthropologists, however they call themselves *Paiter* which means "The true people; ourselves" (cf. <www.paiter.org>, date of access: 29/05/2016).

In the case of the Zoró group, the Surui group gave them the name "Zoró". The name has a pejorative meaning although the Surui people do not explain its meaning further. The self-designation of this group is *Pangejej*. Similarly, the name Karaja is not the group's self-designation. Its meaning is an approximation of "big monkey", from historical sources of the sixteenth and seventeenth centuries. The name of this people in the Karaja language is *Iny*, which means "we". The Juruna people, who live in Xingu Park, were called *Juruna*, which means "black mouth", by another indigenous group, as well. The Juruna instead call themselves *Yudjá*; these people have a division of two human groups: the *Abi* (indigenous people who speak Juruna and were the first navigators of the Xingu River) and *Karai* (non-indigenous people). Currently, in Xingu Park, all indigenous people use the term *Karaiba* to refer to non-indigenous persons.

In the specific case of Kaiabi, the first direct mention of the group was found in a document written in 1850, with the publication of reports of the French traveler Francis de Castelnau. In 1844, Castelnau was in the town Diamantino, Mato Grosso, where he interviewed Apiaká Indians and travelers who visited the area of the Arinos and Teles Pires rivers. These interviews described a "hostile tribe", referred to in the text as Cajah. Thereafter, several other documents refer to Kaiabi, using different spellings for the name: Cajah, Cajaba, Kajabi, Caiabis, Cayabi, Kayabi, etc. Currently, the Indian teachers have decided on the spelling Kaiabi. In any case, it is not the self-designation of the group. Georg Grünberg, an ethnographer who researched the Kaiabi in the 1960s, suggested that the self-designated term is *Iputunuun*, which means something like "our people" (cf. <http://pib.socioambiental.org/pt/povo/kaiabi/271>, date of access: 29/05/2016).

The Prepori's story explains the designation Kaiabi. The Kaiabi group, in a mythological narrative, was born from the seed of the kaja fruit (a tropical fruit of the Northeast and the Midwest regions of Brazil). Prepori said: "We were born from the seed of the kaja". The non-indigenous people came from outside the region and began to call them by this name, by a phonetic approximation that he tries to show in speech: *"... White man came and began to speak kaja, kaja, kaja, kaja, kaia kaia, kaia ... kaiabi."* Although the origin of this name has been lost in time, Prepori's speech put together a mythic narrative with the contact with non-indigenous people. This is based on the principle of "Otherness": to be Kaiabi, it is necessary to be understood in relation to another group that comes from outside the region, i.e. the non-indigenous. This movement creates tension regarding the politics of identity for these people, especially when confronting the question of schooling and writing in the indigenous Kaiabi language. I intend to explore this tension here, beginning with the assignment of names for Kaiabi numbers. First, I will present the story of the Kaiabi group's arrival in Xingu Indigenous Park.

The indigenous group Kaiabi has lived in the park since the 1960s, when they moved from their traditional lands because of constant conflicts and the massacres perpetuated by invading rubber extractors. The invasion on extractive and agricultural fronts, and the successive peace initiatives undertaken by the government agency for Indian affairs (Serviço de Proteção aos Indios) as well as the mission of Prelazia Diamantina, led to the retreat and concentration of the population that remained following the fights and massacres in the area between the Peixe and Teles Pires rivers. Among this population, various Kaiabi families moved to the Indigenous Xingu Park between 1955 and 1966 to escape the plight of penury and persecution in which they found themselves (Franchetto, 1987).

When the Kaiabi group moved to Xingu Park, many things were left behind including the cemeteries of their ancestors, the raw material for the manufacture of sieves with a specific type of design, wood for their bows and a certain type of bamboo for arrows. After they came to Xingu Park, the Kaiabi population increased, as did the number of their villages. Unlike other peoples of the park, who live in large circular villages, Kaiabi prefer small villages scattered along the river, formed by family groups of one or more related families (Franchetto, 1987). For those who do not know the Xingu, Xingu Park is usually associated with the images propagated by the media, such as the major festivals held in the Upper Xingu region. This emphasis on people of Upper Xingu is because these groups look like "pure indigenous persons" as seen from the perspective of the non-indigenous (in terms of appearance, style, utensils etc.). It is common to see a picture of an indigenous person from Upper Xingu to depict the theme of "indigenous culture".

Senra (1996), an anthropologist who worked at the Lower Xingu, narrates a scene about the arrival of two journalists from Discovery Channel TV who were producing a film about Xingu Park:

> Although they had descended into Diauarum Post, an area of broadly speaking Kaiabi influence, they did not express interest in the group. They went to Upper Xingu the next day ... the British proved quite aware that they were looking for stereotypes. Personally, they considered it equally important to make a movie with the Kaiabi, however, they argued that the same could not be said for the television executives or the viewers. (Senra, 1996, pp. 57–58)

The image of "traditional indigenous culture" attributed to peoples of the Upper Xingu has an influence on the Kaiabi people, which represent the highest density, about 700 people, of a population that did not previously inhabit the region. For Kaiabi, according to Senra, the people from Upper Xingu have been representative of "an ancient tradition, which belonged to their ancestors" (Senra, 1996, p. 56). However, despite this contrast with peoples of the Upper Xingu, the Kaiabi have engaged in a process of searching for cultural revitalization through means other than the news in order to conceive and portray the idea of being indigenous.

The Kaiabi group played an important role in the administration of Xingu Park because they had greater contact with the surrounding society and a greater knowledge of Portuguese. The Kaiabi people have stood out in the ways they have sought to assert their identity as distinct from other groups in the Xingu. For the Kaiabi, it is important to distinguish themselves from the surrounding society and from other peoples in the Park. The discursive practices of Kaiabi teachers about the math book in their indigenous language related to ethnic identity. This occurred in relation to numbers in their indigenous language, through which the Kaiabi teachers marked an identity and a political position against the dominant decimal system. For this discussion, it is important to understand the meaning of "numbers" in both Kaiabi culture and practices arising from contact with non-indigenous society.

Numbers for the Kaiabi Math Book

Originally, the Kaiabi's terminology for numbers in their native language only went up to five. To indicate larger amounts, fingers and toes were used, for example for counting the number of days of hunters stayed in the forest. For stays of more than twenty days, the moon, which for the Kaiabi has three phases, did the marking: Jay ruwi (new moon), Owauramu (full moon) and Ikuejowamu (when the moon appears on both sides). Currently, Kaiabi teachers are writing numerical terms as follows: 1 – *ajepeitee;* 2 – *mukui;* 3 – *muapyt;* 4 – *irupawe;* 5 – *irupawe irue'em.* The fact that there is no name for larger numbers does not imply that the Kaiabi people do not use numbers greater than five. The difference relates to the objective with which the number is used, either as a time marker, as in the example cited above, or to produce drawings of weaving, as will be explained below.

The Kaiabi produce artisanally woven baskets (*yrupem* – see Fig. 2) using 15 patterns different patterns of incremental difficulty, which are learnt in a particular order. The drawings that appear on the twisted baskets depict the mythical narratives of the group (Ribeiro, 1986). In order to learn the design patterns, the first to be learned is named I'yp, i.e. number 1.

Fig. 2: Yrupem (photographed by the author)

When I was in the community following the research undertaken by an indigenous teacher on Kaiabi baskets, I asked him about the initial formation of twisted baskets. In relation to basket number one, I asked how they know the exact number of strips to the top of the braid. The teacher pointed to the drawing and said that the form shows how to make the design. Afterwards, I asked about the number of strips in a vertical position. Instantly, the Kaiabi teacher counted one by one and said "seventeen". Then I asked him: "How? If the Kaiabi only have numbers up to five?" Very quietly, the teacher replied that from the strip center (symmetrically), he counted on each side: three, three, and two (Figs 3 and 4).

Indeed, even though Kaiabi numerical terms do not go beyond five, there is a way of organizing quantities by sorting groups of three, four,

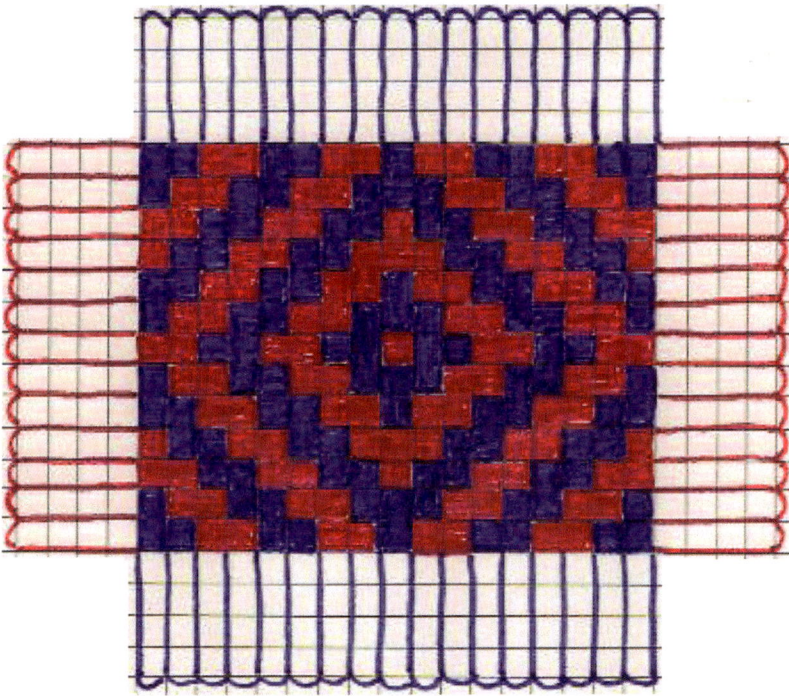

Fig. 3: Example from the math textbook made in collaboration with the indigenous teachers (photographed by the author)

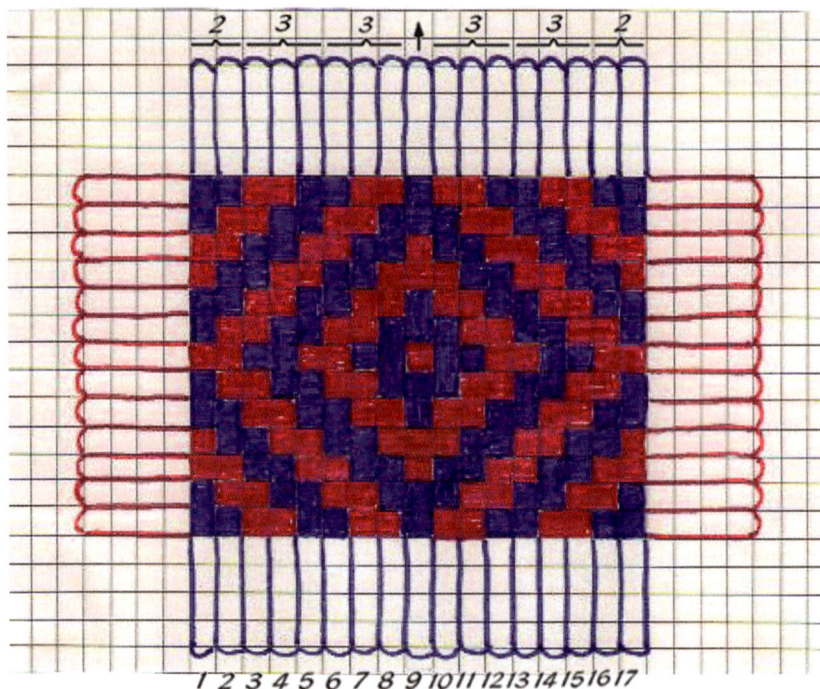

Fig. 4: I'yp (photographed by the author)

or two. In this context, the practices relate to Kaiabi quantification, and
certainly not to the idea of counting towards the accumulation of large
quantities. Counting has another purpose. In the case of weaving, counting
is expected to produce a particular design and for this, the use of clusters is
sufficient without the need for a verbal description for the total amount of
strips. With social contact with non-Indian society, mainly through trade,
came new practices that now require the use of terms that designate larger
numbers. The goal of using numbers in this context is the need to enumerate
larger amounts and is also associated with the concept of monetary value.

An issue arises in relation to the use of indigenous languages and the
Portuguese language for such practices. For these purposes, some new terms
were created in the indigenous language. With regard to using money, for
example, the following terms are used: *Ka'aranuu* means money (it literally

translates as paper); *Owuumaʾe* (large note, or large leaf) used for bills of denominations fifty and one hundred; *Owiimaʾe* (small note, or small leaf) used for bills of ten and one; *Yʾwypeʾi* (coins or round pods). To give meaning to numerical values introduced by social contact, terms were used in new ways in the indigenous language, designating larger or smaller values in monetary terms. Changes in social activities have put the Kaiabi people into contact with another numerical universe that has been incorporated into their daily practices. This occurred as commercial practices became part of Kaiabi life, and cannot be seen exclusively as a non-indigenous activity. These new practices in this new numerical universe are already part of Kaiabi life.

When the idea of developing a mathematics textbook was first presented to indigenous teachers, the Kaiabi teachers immediately showed an interest in having such didactic material. All groups participating in the course opted to write a book in their indigenous language, including the Kaiabi teachers. However, the use of Portuguese for larger numbers created an obstacle, both symbolic and political in nature, in producing the math book in the indigenous language. Nevertheless, some Kaiabi teachers claimed to have an "indigenous mathematics", one of them said that they use "a lot of math" when they build a house, but "it's very difficult to put this knowledge in the math book". Another Kaiabi teacher said:

> We want an indigenous Kaiabi math book. We want a book for working with students in our own Indigenous mathematical language [...] how will we put in the book the indigenous way of doing mathematics? We have a lot of math, which we use when a person builds a home, makes a hammock and an arrow.

We can observe, in the Kaiabi teacher's remarks above, a discourse of defense in relation to an "indigenous mathematics" that is related to a "mathematical language". It is important to highlight that the discussion about different number conventions stems from the contact between the Kaiabi people and dominant culture. This intercultural encounter produced a discourse of defending and maintaining the Kaiabi's own "mathematical language". With a view to achieving this aim, the Kaiabi teachers decided to hold a meeting with leaders and elders to discuss an expansion of the numerical terminology in the Kaiabi language. Following the discussion, an indigenous teacher turned to me and said with a smile: "Now we can talk about any number: one hundred, two hundred, three hundred ....".[2] They had approved an expansion of their numerical terminology up to the number ten.

Whilst the expansion of the numerical terminology proposed by the Kaiabi group represents the imposition of a dominant system, it also reveals characteristics of this community's sense of numbers. One such conception is to rely on groups of three, four, or two. The linguistic structure of the proposed terms after five, is based on the idea of organizing groups:

1   *ajepeitee*
2   *mukui*
3   *muapyt*
4   *irupawe* (iru = partner)
5   *irupawe irue 'em* (i.e. two partners and one is alone)
6   *muapyriru* (i.e. three partners)
7   *muapyrirue'em* (i.e. three partners and one is alone)
8   *irupawepawe* (i.e. four plus four partners)
9   *muapyjuejue* (i.e. three is repeated three times)
10 *ae po jawe* (i.e. this is the same number as all of the fingers on our hands)

The emphasis on idea of numerical terms approved at the assembly has a symbolic character. The expansion of terminology has reinforced the affirmation of the group's identity. The ability to use larger numbers in the Kaiabi language implies that the group is not placed in an inferior position in relation to non-indigenous mathematics and to other indigenous people, as is evident from the teacher's comment that "Now we can talk about any number: one hundred, two hundred, three hundred ... ".

---

2   All quotes stem from the author's fieldnotes or interviews with the research participants. They have been translated into English by the author.

Indigenous Schooling and Identity Politics

This movement around the Kaiabi math book and, in particular, the numerical terms in their native language, is part of an identity politics through which the Kaiabi's identity is (re)constructed in interactions with indigenous and non-indigenous people. When they say that "now we can talk about any number: one hundred, two hundred, three hundred ...", although it appears to be a contradictory discourse because the extension was made based on the dominant system, the Kaiabi teachers appropriated this system by creating a new names for these numbers. Despite following a decimal system, the proposal maintains a notion of groups inherent to the Kaiabi's sense of number. For example, one teacher suggested that the Kaiabi word for number 16 should be *ajeipeei muapyriru* (one (ten) and three pairs). The reading of number 16 focuses on the digits but retains the Kaiabi sense of number, i.e. six is seen as three groups of two.

The decimal system came from social contact with the non-indigenous world, however it became part of the Kaiabi's daily life. In an interview with a Kaiabi teacher, he said that before this expansion of numerical terminology, they borrowed numerical terms from Portuguese to express larger numbers:

TARUPI: It is important that we have more numbers for counting, you understand? Because at the moment, we are only counting in a non-indigenous way, and that isn't good, you know. So we have to have more numbers ... eh ... to go higher, because our counting is very low.

JACKIE: And why do you think that you need to use larger numbers in the Kaiabi indigenous language?

TARUPI: Ah, so ... we need larger numbers in order to use our own numbers when speaking with our relatives; We have to speak the same language.

JACKIE: With relatives.

TARUPI: Yes, with relatives. At the moment we speak in indigenous language about everything, but when we have to speak about numbers, we say the numbers in Portuguese.

JACKIE: That is, when you're talking to a relative, when you have to say a number, you ...

TARUPI: The language of numbers is the white man's language.

JACKIE: You speak in Portuguese.

TARUPI: It's not good, you know. Now, if we have a number that we could say in our language and when counting, just say the number in our own language – that would be important for us, you know. But if we depend on the white man's language, we will never get our own high numbers, you know.

To borrow "non-indigenous language" to express numbers means to speak in a non-indigenous language and is the same as perpetuating a dependent relationship which can be expressed in the following claim: "if we depend only on the white man's (non-indigenous) language, we never get our own high numbers". The construction of new terms for these numbers in the native language is part of a broader effort to affirm the Kaiabi's identity. The number is no longer "white man's (non-indigenous)" language and becomes "indigenous" language, or the "Kaiabi" language. In a broader context of new practices introduced in the Kaiabi's daily life the way in which they affirmed their ethnic identity, changed by portraying these numbers as no longer the "white man's (non-indigenous)" language, but the "Kaiabi's" language.

Maher (1996, 2010) explores the various facets of indigenous teachers' identities, and how the indigenous language in its oral and written forms has been a major factor in the reconstruction of these identities. As he argues, the (inventing of) writing of indigenous languages has played a major role in the assertion of ethnic identities, as it has in the formation of other identities: the indigenous historians and the indigenous researchers. Thus, to Maher, discourse plays a key role in asserting distinct indigenous identities. In the case of Kaiabi teachers, this assertion of an ethnic identity arose from writing numbers for a math book in their indigenous language – also turning school into a place of on-going change, where the indigenous teachers assume the role of *translators*. They have to move between two worlds in a continuous movement of identity building.

To conclude, the colonial model of education historically built for indigenous people now faces *interculturalism* as a new paradigm. In the context of bilingual and intercultural indigenous education, indigenous languages and Portuguese have played an important role in relation to the formation of ethnic identities. Identity formation takes place in a *minority* context, in defense of a symbolic political territory and for the maintenance of cultural meanings, customs, and practices distinct to other meanings and practices held by the *majority* of society. However, this process of building an indigenous textbook reveals a place marked by blurred borders constituted by tension, difference, and hybrid identities.

In the case of the Kaiabi people, speaking Portuguese is a historical and political need, and the intercultural contact is given. Thus, they have to deal with this identity reinvention process all the time. The subjects, who emerge from a process of intercultural contact, are engaged in identity politics and in a reinvention of Kaiabi identity by means of relating to knowledge and cultural practices that are produced and reconstructed through the intercultural contact. Intercultural encounters can be understood, from a post-colonial view, not as a mixture of two homogeneous cultures that generates a hybrid, but as the coexistence of two or more heterogeneous cultures, without a harmonious fusion. Such coexistence is always marked by ambiguity, tension without an end ...

References

Balloco, A. E. (2006). A escrita e o escrito: Produzindo identidades e domesticando diferenças. In B. Mariani (Ed.), *A escrita e os escritos: Reflexões em análise do discurso e psicanálise* (pp. 81–108). São Carlos: Clara Luz.

Bhabha, H. K. (1994). *The Location of culture*. New York: Routledge.

Cavalcanti, M., & Maher, T. J. M. (1993). Interação transcultural na formação do professor indio. In L.Seki (Ed.), *Interação índio/não-índio no limiar do século XXI* (pp. 217–230). Campinas: Unicamp.

Fairclough, N. (1992). *Discourse and social change*. Cambridge: Polity Press.

Franchetto, B. (1987). *Laudo antropológico: A ocupação indígena de região dos formadores e do alto curso do Rio Xingu*. (Anthropological report), Cuiabá: OPAN/CIMI.

Hall, S. (1997). *Representation: Cultural representations and signifying practices*. London: Sage/Open University.

Kontopodis, M., & Matera, V. (2010). Doing memory, doing identity: Politics of the everyday in contemporary global communities. *Outlines: Critical Practice Studies*, 12(2), 1–14.

Maher, T. J. M. (1996). *Ser professor sendo índio: questões de língua(gem) e identidade.* (Unpublished doctoral dissertation). Campinas: University of Campinas.

Maher, T. J. M. (2010). Políticas linguísticas e políticas de identidade: currículo e representações de professores indígenas na Amazônia Ocidental Brasileira, *Currículo sem Fronteiras*, 10(1), 33–48.

Mendes, J. R. (2001). *Ler, escrever e contar: Práticas de numeramento-letramento no contexto de formação de professores do parque indígena do Xingu* (Unpublished doctoral dissertation). Campinas: University of Campinas.

Ministério da Educação (1998). *Referencial curricular para as escolas indígenas.* Brasília: Ministério da Educação.

Ribeiro, B. (1986). Desenhos semânticos e identidade étnica: O caso Kaiabi. In D. Ribeiro (Ed.), *Suma Etnológica Brasileira, v. 3* (pp. 265–286). Petropolis: Vozes/ FINEP.

Senra, K. (1996). Os Kaiabi. In S. Athayde, & G. Silva (Ed), *Bases socioambientais para o desenvolvimento de alternativas econômicas sustentáveis na região norte do parque indígena do Xingu* (pp. 50–78). Mato Grosso: Instituto Socioambiental/ISA.

Woodward, K. (1997). *Identity and difference.* London: Sage/The Open University.

ANA LUIZA BUSTAMANTE SMOLKA, LAVÍNIA LOPES SALOMÃO
MAGIOLINO, ELIZABETH DOS SANTOS BRAGA & ANA LUCIA
HORTA NOGUEIRA

5. "Special" and "Normal" in Students' Voices: Meaning Production at a State-Funded School in Campinas

Cultural Development as Appropriation of Social Practices

Throughout the twentieth century many attempts took place to explore, conceptualize, and evaluate *development*. In such different fields of knowledge as biology, psychology, history, sociology, and economy, one can find diverse ways of conceiving, referring to, and studying this heterogeneous notion and phenomenon. At the same time, reactions to the term, criticism of its idea, and questioning, displacements, and deconstruction of this very notion have also marked the debates on development (Henriques, Hollway, Urwin, Venn & Walkerdine, 1984; Burman, 1994; Danzinger, 1990).

Indeed, the word *development* mobilizes historically produced images, meanings, and senses, which are inscribed in our everyday practices and mark our common modes of seeing and interpreting people's actions, behaviors, gestures, and words. In the word *development*, we find some deeply interwoven and implicated meaning that resonated in our current uses of the term: *to reveal, to take out of the wrapping, to let the inside appear; to unfold; growth, maturation; increment, accumulation; improvement, perfection; orientation to, finality, teleology; temporal order, linearity; progress, progression; period, stage; normal, normality; evolution; movement, change; genesis, emergence; revolution, involution; transformation; discontinuity, heterogeneity ...*

In such a frame of reference, any conceptual elaboration implies a (trans-) formation and a dialectical movement that brings the *old* in the *new*. To be aware of this movement does not minimize, but situates, the historical relevance of conceptualization work. A concept carries in itself a history of the use of the word, as Vygotsky comments (1934/1987, p. 241). Development is a word that appears with extraordinary frequency throughout Vygotsky's works. In the *Genesis of Higher Mental Functions*, he warns:

> [...] we must elucidate the very concept of development as we have done in the chapters on the analysis and structure of higher mental processes. The fact is that because of the crisis in psychology, all concepts have become meaningless and vague. They change depending on the investigators' point of view. In different systems of psychology based on different methodological principles, all the fundamental categories of research, including that of genesis, acquire different meanings. (Vygotsky, 1929/1981, p. 147)

It is interesting to note that in his search for a conceptual clarification, Vygotsky's uses and meanings of the term *development* did vary in relation to a specific focus or object at issue, and they did change in the course of his theoretical elaborations: *"the human being develops"*, *"the child develops"*, *"higher mental functions develop"*, *"language develops"*, *"concepts develop"*, *"word meaning develops"*, *"personality develops"*, *"emotions develop"*...[1]

When discussing issues related to the status of the sign and the role of meaning in consciousness elaboration, Vygotsky acknowledged: "The most important for us is the development of meanings" (1933–34/1997, p. 134); "The sense of the words is changed by the motive" (1933–34/1997, p. 136); "The word in a context becomes both restricted and enriched; the word absorbs the sense of the contexts" (1933–34/1997, p. 135). Throughout his theoretical elaborations, Vygotsky also gave special emphasis to the *cultural development* of the child, and continually called attention to the *history* of human cultural development. In his ways of approaching human development he consistently and insistently pointed to the *history of development*:

---

[1]   These expressions are taken and shortened from various Vygotsky's works; put together here, they point to the many facets of development (cf. Schneuwly, 2002).

history of the development of the pointing gesture, of the development of human activity, of the development of higher mental functions, of the development of language, of the development of signs, of the development of consciousness (Vygotsky, 1929/1981). In this frame of reference, the individual's *cultural development* is seen as a personal history intrinsically woven into cultural practices and human history.

Vygotsky inquired: "How does the collective create higher mental functions in the child?" (1929/1981, p. 165). This inquiry is pushed forward by asking: How does "culture, as a product of social life and human social activity" constitute human development (Vygotsky, 1929/1981, p. 164)? And how do we assume the consequences and implications of the principle that "human beings produce their very conditions of existence and produce themselves in these conditions"? Here, it seems, we find and forge some other possible meanings of *development*: a) resulting from human interaction and cultural production; b) related to a historical, constitutive feature. As the notions of *human activity, interaction,* and *production* become inscribed in the conception of development, it becomes transformed: human development starts to be conceived as a cultural-historical product(ion).

If collective human activity constitutes human beings, human development is then anchored on the *participation in* and *appropriation of* culture. Education, as the human being's work upon human beings, becomes crucial. The notion of *appropriation* was taken as object of investigation in our previous works (Góes, 1992; Laplane, 2000; Nogueira, 1991; Pino, 1992; Smolka, 1992, 1997, 2000). In the analyses of teaching and knowledge appropriation we have noticed many conflicting meanings related to the (im)possibilities of "appropriativeness": How do children take over, attribute belonging to, make proper, turn pertinent knowledge and practices? How do they develop capacities and means – modes and instruments – for acting? Some modes of participation/appropriation might acquire analytical visibility, while others remain impossible to be traced.

The impossibility of empirically tracing and the difficulty in interpreting, finding, and reading indicators of *appropriation* lead us to reflect upon the theoretical status and strength of Vygotsky's statements concerning the internalization of social practices. In his attempts to understand what makes possible the *conversion* of social relations into individual mental functions, Pino (2000) emphasizes that

> [W]hat is internalized from social relations are not material relations but the meanings they have for people, meanings that emerge in these very relations. To say that what is internalized is the meaning of such relations is equivalent to saying that what is internalized is the meaning the *other* in the relation has for the *I*. [...] In other words, it is through the *other* that the *I* constitutes him/herself as a social being [...]. (Pino, 2000, pp. 66–67, our translation from Portuguese)

Methodological Issues: Signs, Words, Discourse

During the last decades, the researchers from the *Thought and Language Research Group* (GPPL/UNICAMP) have been conducting several research projects in schools and non-formal educational contexts. In these research projects, we have been highlighting *discourse* and *education* as fundamental social practices in the constitution of human thinking. We have inquired about the conditions and dynamics of such practices, attempting to understand: (1) how they become stabilized, instituted, and transformed while affecting the involved subjects; and (2) the modes of participation and constitution of human subjects in the collective process of history, memory, and knowledge production.

As we work in the formal education system, we experience a multitude of issues, problems, tensions, and doubts at the core of our daily school activity. The classroom micro-sphere certainly reflects the contradictions that pervade our contemporary practices. Globalization, information technologies, and instant communication, as well as deep changes in the conditions and relations of production, in work relations and employment, in the social modes of living, and the most varied forms of access to cultural goods and production, human resources and possibilities, certainly do affect and transform human experience – perception, conception – of space, time, and values.

Diversity, complexity, mobility, fluidity, precariousness, inequality, inclusion are some of the terms that have been characterizing our practices (cf. Bauman, 2001; Giddens, 1991; Castells, 1997). Within and at the margins of such global *ambience*, we find that the notion of development, the semiotic dimension, the status of language, the notion of discourse, and ways of teaching, learning, and researching, all demand constant (re-)elaboration. Emphasizing the historical dimension of human development, Vygotsky brought out what he called the *instrumental, double stimulation*, or *experimental-genetic* method. One of his major concerns had to do with the ways of teaching, the ways of studying teaching relations, as well as the results or effects of such relations. In the last period of his life, he stated that "[s]emiotic analysis is the only adequate method for the study of the systemic and semantic structure of consciousness," also affirming that "the word is a microcosm of human the structure consciousness" (Vygotsky, 1933–34/1997, p. 137; 1934/1987, p. 285). His *method* thus escapes from rigidity but not from rigor, pointing to an instigating flexibility, which approximates his efforts to the efforts of many other contemporary authors in different fields. Inspired by Vygotsky's notions and assuming that object and method are built in the process (of investigation), we have been trying to deeply examine the theoretical and empirical implications of such statements.

In order to develop our methodological and analytical procedures, we have constantly questioned and reexamined Vygotskian proposals in dialogue with other contemporary authors. This way of positioning encourages and compels us into academic dialogue with sociologists, linguists, historians, discourse analysts, among others, in an interdisciplinary movement.

We have been relating Vygotsky's inspiring contributions to approaches of ethnographic studies, which also point to the possibilities of taking this kind of methodological research as the locus of inquiry (Green, Dixon & Zaharlick, 2001; Rockwell, 1999; Ezpeleta & Rockwell, 1986; Geertz, 1973). According to this, we have been assuming the possibility of imagining and designing *experimental* (in Vygotskian terms) teaching situations as a locus of learning as well as of investigation. In this process, we have also searched to deepen our understanding of the notions of discourse and social practice. How does discourse relate to the material conditions which have engendered it (cf. Henriques, Hollway, Urwin, Venn & Walkerdine, 1984)?

Discussing human development within historical cultural conditions, we argue that a key to understanding the constitution of human subjects in/through social/societal relations is in the way of conceiving the production of signs and meanings in the material conditions of existence. We consider that Vygotsky's and Bakhtin's elaborations at the intersection of different issues and areas of investigation produce a conceptual core which makes viable new modes of understanding *signification* as human activity, of *discourse* as social practice.

Thus, assuming that the verbal form of language is a historical product(ion) of human activity, which became the most powerful *means* (instrument/constitutive mode) in the organization of mental functioning and social practices, we highlight and relate *school practices* and *discourse practices* as the objects and loci of our empirical research. We take them as *instituted and constituting practices* resultant from social relations, produced in/through the always transforming material conditions of existence.

Exploring School Practices: Our Empirical Field

Since 2005, our research team has carried out research and intervention projects in a Brazilian public i.e. state-funded elementary school located in a suburban area in the northern part of Campinas, the second major city in the State of São Paulo. The researchers (university professors, graduate and undergraduate students) have a long relationship with this school and participate weekly in school activities. The school district adjoins two other municipal areas: the well-to-do Paulinia and the impoverished Sumaré. It is currently a neighborhood surrounded by industries, warehouses, and small areas of agricultural cultivation. It is an area of intense migratory movement.

The population in the region can be mainly divided into two categories: one composed of small local merchants, officers, and secretaries with a more comfortable economic situation; and another of less favored employees, laborers, farm workers, and servants, among others. A significant number of families live on social benefits, and many others survive through informal activity. The scarcity of public facilities is a feature of the neighborhood: there are only two nursery schools, the closest health center is six kilometers away, and public transportation is precarious. In 2005, while this empirical work was done, the school was attended by 700 elementary education students, from 1st through 8th grades, plus adult education, in four four-hour shifts (7.00 to 11.00; 11.00 to 15.00; 15.00 to 19.00; 19.00 to 23.00).

At that time, a team of teachers of this school decided to introduce an alternative pedagogical project for a group of fifteen 6th grade (13 to 16-year-old) students who had been exhibiting, according to the teachers' evaluation, learning and behavior problems. Invited by the teachers to support and to join the project, the researchers[2] participated in the interactions of students and teachers in the classroom and within the broader school context.

This *alternative teaching project* was called into being after teachers had identified the following problems: 1) the large deficit presented by these students regarding knowledge in diverse subject areas; 2) the students' advanced age for the regular school process; and 3) their probable low self-esteem, fruit of many years of school experience without much success. The project had as specific objectives: 1) to deepen the knowledge of the students' reality; 2) to reconstruct their self-esteem; 3) to renew their interest and respect for school; 4) to provide means for the development of reading and writing abilities. In order to reach these objectives, the teachers proposed interdisciplinary work with a reduced number of students.[3]

We will bring to discussion here two empirical situations from this same group of students within the public school setting that, considered in

---

2   The following researchers participated in the field work: Lavínia Lopes Salomão Magiolino and Daniela Dias dos Anjos, graduate students; Aline Caprera, Thelma Anacleto Belo dos Santos, and Ricardo Noronha, undergraduate students; Ana Lucia Horta Nogueira, university professor; Ana Luiza B. Smolka, head of research group. The research group was larger than this project group. Other scholars took part in the analysis and discussions of empirical material.

3   Extracted from the text of the teachers' project proposal, translated from Portuguese by the author.

relation to one another, allow for interesting points of debate. In proceeding through an analysis of these two situations we attempt to explore *means and modes of appropriation* of practices related to cultural development.

Situation 1: "Special" within the Institutional Setting

The principal[4] (PR) of the school is talking with the students while they are waiting for the geography teacher. The students are quite restless, demanding to go outside. The PR argues that they are only messing around. The conversation continues to a point when somebody mentions that this is a special (education) class. The PR contests this and refers to a previous meeting with parents, when the project was presented and explained to them. The students argue back, saying that this class is different, that *this kind of project is indeed special.* The PR argues that all classes have projects.

ST1:	[starts screaming]: So, why can't we go out as the other classes do? 'Cause we are special!
PR:	The others cannot go either ...
ST1:	Then why don't we have lessons with Ma and Li [teachers]? [The PR tries to argue that the teachers choose their schedule.]
ST1:	Chose!! Chose!! [with indignation] Nobody chose this class!! And look! Look at this number of (so few) students!!! Is this a classroom!?
ST1:	Look, look at this task we have to do!!! [He shows the task in the notebooks]
ST1:	Isn't that special!? Everything is so easy!! Just English [ESL] we learn!!! We have lessons from the 5th grade!
ST2:	Yeah! In 6th grade we have lessons from the 5th, in 7th, from the 6th ... at the end we know nothing!

If the team of teachers was attentive and careful in their proposal, if they jointly considered and analysed the students' situation; if they chose to

---

4   We are using abbreviated designations in our transcriptions: ST – student; TE – teacher; PR – principal.

design and implement the project; how can we understand the students' comments? How is this *feeling*, this *effect* of "special education" produced in spite of the teachers' pondering and emphatic negations[5] of such meaning? How does this meaning impose itself, contrary to the teachers' intentions and objectives? An analysis of the students' utterances highlights some of their arguments:

1. The restricted number of students in the class: *Look at this number of (so few) students!!! Is this a classroom!?*
2. The kinds of tasks, demands, lessons: *Look, look at the work we have to do!!! [He shows the works in the notebooks] We have lessons from the 5th grade!!*
3. The features of the proposed activities which seem to confirm the incapacity the teachers attribute to the students, in spite of their being older: *Everything is so easy!! Isn't that special!??*
4. The images they have of other teachers whom they consider more rigorous: *Then why don't we have lessons with Ma and Li?*
5. The lack of teaching, the lack of knowledge: *In 6th grade we have lessons from the 5th, in 7th, from the 6th ... at the end we know nothing!*

The students' arguments indicate an *interplay of images* that operates in sense production: images the students have of a regular classroom, images they have of their group at the moment; images of what is being taught; images they have of themselves; images they have of the teachers; images the teachers have of the students and what they are able to learn; images the teachers have of the object of knowledge; and so on.

The teachers' written proposal makes explicit some of these images:

During the lessons in the last school year ... these students ... showed their interest in being at school to be playing, dating, fighting, dancing, etc. ... presented learning difficulties ... their interest in playing and group interaction ... turn(ed) classes quite uninteresting and stressful ...[6]

---

5   In other situations we followed some of the teachers' arguments reiterating that the students were indeed "quite special," although they emphasized a positive meaning.

6   Extracted from the teachers' project, translated from Portuguese by the authors.

Large deficits, advanced age, low self-esteem, learning difficulties, history of failure, divergent interests, inadequate behavior, sources of stress compose the most *common* images of the referred students who compose the group. Indeed, uncountable moments of teasing, provoking, mocking, ironical comments, seduction, rap singing, dancing, fighting were *proper* to the students' ways of interacting.

But different meanings and interpretations of such behaviors configured their *(im-)pertinence* or *(in-)appropriatedness* at the school setting. For most of the teachers, they did not seem to fit the school genre. At the same time, by establishing as criteria for inclusion in the group the fact that the students were older or "over-aged," this aspect (developmental indicator) did not seem to reflect on the teachers' practices: they did not change the proposed tasks (e.g.: coloring the star, drawing heroes, and the like), which were considered by the students to be childish activities that also did not fit the *appropriate* school genre for their age. The teachers' conscious choices and arguments for the group composition reiterated, indeed constituted, the very *special* condition of these students.

These images and (pre-) conceptions became constitutive of students' and teachers' modes of inter-acting. Students' and teachers' images, conceptions. and expectations coincided in a *space of differences* (Bourdieu, 1994) marked by distinct positions, experiences, and points-of-view. They became inscribed in school practices, integrated into a *habitus*, and produced effects independently of the subjects' conscious intentions. Images and discourse, images *in* discourse, operate in the production of what Bourdieu et. al. (1997) call the *specific efficacy of schooling*, where *forms of hidden exclusion* take place.

Modes of appropriation – appropriation of culture, appropriation of knowledge, appropriation of meanings, appropriation of words – can be seen as a function of these relations and positions. Features of proper or improper behavior, adequate or inadequate contents, emerge as *the results* of such positions and relations. They might become pertinent or not within and in relation to a specific sphere or *genre of activity* (Clot, 2006). An individual might "*turn proper*" or "*make his own*" social resources in a non-suitable way for others, in a not-necessarily-conventionalized way

(Smolka, 2000). Yet, what is or becomes *ap-propriated* (proper i.e. pertinent, adequate, suitable) by and for human subjects in interaction with each other is related to the *signification* – multiple and diverse meanings – produced in the complex institutional relations.

Amidst so many (non-) coincidences in the school context, the word *special* is used in quite heterogeneous senses. Indeed, it condenses different meanings and feelings related to reciprocal (in-) adequate behaviors and expectations. It appears as an *arena of struggle* (Voloshinov & Bakhtin, 1973). Its meanings for the involved human subjects are produced in the dynamics of teaching relations in a history of school practices.

Situation II: The "Normal" Conditions of Living

In the second month of classes, one of the ways the geography teacher chose to introduce a specific topic was to invite the students to observe and describe the environment around the school, looking through the classroom window. She was a substitute teacher for the year and not previously acquainted with the group of teachers, students, or surrounding neighborhood. She asked the students to describe the neighborhood, to identify commercial and industrial activities, to comment on work relations, life conditions, and quality of life. From these talks and issues, the students entered into an argument with the teacher and started insistently asking her to watch the film *City of God* at school.[7]

7　The film is based on a novel written by Paulo Lins, a young photographer and journalist who lived in the "planned" neighborhood called Cidade de Deus, to which the inhabitants of a whole slum in Rio de Janeiro were moved in the 1960s. The film (*Cidade de Deus*, 2002, directed by Fernando Meirelles and Kátia Lund) shows the features and changes in life quality through the years.

Having joined the teaching project in spite of not being able to participate in its planning, the geography teacher took the students' demand to the teachers' team. After 6 months, almost at the end of the school year, the film was finally shown to the students at school, with cuts of sexual and violent scenes. The students noticed the cuts and many left the classroom, refusing to watch the film or to participate in the following discussions. At the moment of discussion, the geography teacher, the teachers' adviser, 5 students, and 2 researchers were present in the classroom. This group had two video cameras, one operated by the students, another by the researchers. Three pieces of the transcribed 45-minute talk will be the object of our considerations here:

Fragment 1:

1   TE: We are talking about a very serious issue here, but what is worrying me is this question: why did you want ... you looked for this film ... to tell me something ...

2   ST3: Yeah, teacher, it is for everybody to see the truth.

3   ST4: Yeah, the truth!

4   ST5: Yeah!

5   ST3: The truth, brother!

6   ST5: Yeah! 'Cause there are teachers who tell us like this: 'Write about your life' ... and then ... do not even believe ...

7   ST4: Teachers who think ... when we fight we rebel because of the school. It is not because of the school ... we do not stand around the neighborhood, the world out there ... The school, the world around ... everything is the same ... the film is showing what we go through outside, how it is outside ...

8   ST3: Yeah, teacher, this film, it is almost the same thing ...

9   ST5: It is all the same thing ...

Fragment 2:

1   TE: Why did you want to watch City of God?

2   ST3: 'Cause it is real life, this film! It does exist. It shows what exists ... slang ...

3   TE: But just for that you wanted to bring this film to school?

4   ST3: No, cause it is real life!

5   TE: And the school is not real life?

   (...)

6   ST3: ... here who kills dies, isn't that so, Jon? So ...

7   TE: What do you mean, who kills dies!?

   (...)

8   ST3: Yeah, brother, if [you] do not go to jail, [you] die!

9   TE: Tell me a little bit more of this story.

10 ST5: ... the guys selling arms, drugs ...

11 ST3: Yeah, brother. Gosh, brother! The guy dying with 30 bullets. How come ...

12 ST5: Innocent people ...

13 ST4: ... owes 10 reais, 5 reais, the next day is dead.

Fragment 3:

1   ST3: Both sides steal ... no way out ... Even the rich ...

2   TEA: And how is it to live in a society like this? How?

3   ST3: Normal.

4   TE: Normal?

   (silence)

5   TE: Normal, Van? Normal, Pam?

6   ST3: Ah! Teacher, in this neighborhood here, you don't need to expect anything. Everything has happened already ...

7   TE: In this neighborhood?

8   ST3: Everything has happened already ...

9   TE: Jon, is it normal?

10 ST4: (moves his head, affirming)

11 TE: Everybody steals? Rich, poor ... is that so?

12 ST4: (moves head affirming)

13 ST3: ... I think the rich people started to steal and then the poor people saw it was ok and they started to do it also ...

14 TE: Girls ... Pam ...?

15 ST5 Normal.

   (translated from Portuguese by the authors)

We could use here a plethora of concepts, constructs, and analytical instruments from many different fields of knowledge. Indeed, we have been making a number of attempts in our "looking/interpreting exercises," in our approaches to the empirical material. What do the students refer to when

they talk about *real* life, or *normal* life? How does school participate in
the students' living experiences? What are the possible contours of "real"
or "normal" in contemporary practices? Thus we focus on discourse,
attempting to give visibility to concrete conditions of learning and
development.

The teacher opens the discussion by asking the students *why* they
wanted to watch the film at school. If almost all students had already
watched it, and if the teachers had too, one issue becomes: why watch
the film *together at school*? To look through the window was one of the
teacher's strategic resources to orient the students' modes of looking at
their own reality. She wanted to re-dimension the students' experiences and
points-of-view. Her way of seeing was oriented by her knowledge – didactic, scientific – marked by social commitment. The teacher calls attention
to the environment and highlights forms of human activity, relations and
practices. The street, the traffic in various directions, people walking; buses,
cars, trucks; population in movement: this concerns geography! And she
proceeds, conceptualizing transport, urbanization, industry, and commerce.

The students in turn show an understanding of the teacher's talk, but
they contest and argue with her, speaking from another point of view, a
different social position. The students' way of looking is oriented by their
living experience and their knowledge of certain practices they experiences
daily. For the students, to talk about urbanization, transport, and commerce
is to talk about the concrete conditions of life, about what affects them each
and every day, and that means to talk about drug traffic, bargaining and
intimidation, power relations and restriction of spaces, murders, death ...
It is to talk about common practices, of what is commonly practiced in
the closer community.

We could say that the film was suggested as the students' resource to
orient the teacher's way of looking. It was a mode of making legitimate their
ways of speaking, their ways of living; a strategy to show a real, normal,
daily world. For the students, it was important that the teacher could see
what they are used to see, how they are used to live; the teacher could feel
what they are used to feel.

The students resort to the filmic narrative as a way of making legitimate
the discredited narrative of their own lives:

- Yeah! 'Cause there are teachers who tell us like this: 'Write about your life' ... and then ... do not even believe ... (Fragment 1, turn 6)
- The film is showing what we go through outside, how it is outside ... (Fragment 1, turn 7)
- It is all the same thing ... (Fragment 1, turn 9)
- It is real life, this film! (Fragment 2, turn 2).

The students' statements mobilize fundamental questions related to the ways of living and speaking about their lives. After all, what concerns *real* life? And *normal* ways of living? How do we speak about life? The film appears as a possibility – a resource, a strategy, an occasion, a condition, a mode – of talking about life. As human production, the filmic narrative reflects, refracts, pervades, and affects human subjectivity and reality. Nonetheless, it is based on a written narrative, a novel produced from lived, related, disseminated experiences from many subjects in interaction with each other. The weaving of talks and narratives points to some concrete conditions of life that configure common, habitual, normal, natural contemporary living. Different social positions highlighted in the discourse – rich people, poor people – coincide in the practice of a common action: stealing. Concrete, material conditions turn into *normal* conditions. Features of normality, naturalness, seem to become installed without being questioned.

The students could have related their experience to the abundant daily news. But here, the *means* make a difference. The filmic narrative, as a work of art, acquires a specific, mobilizing, and effective function. The students find in the film a narrative (which appears consistent with their *experience*) of living. They share with the protagonists the same conditions, same plot. The one who lives and the one who narrates become (con-)fused. They make the narrative of the other *their own*. The narrative of the *other* coincides with what *I* wanted to narrate of my own life. (My) life becomes a novel, turns into a film. Ways of narrating and ways of representing life through words are woven through the *image-in-action*. One's words affect, resonate in the other's consciousness (Bakhtin, 1984). The experience of the "I" in isolation can be shared and collectively re-dimensioned by the consciously elaborated experience of "we". This re-dimensioning changes the meanings, the status of lived experience, the strength of arguments.

In the movement of *appropriating* (turning proper, making their own) the content of geography presented by the teacher, the students find a *proper* way of telling about the neighborhood, anchored on partially *alien* words and images. The film becomes a possible *locus of the objectification of images and practices*. The weaving of narratives seems to confirm a *normal*, a *natural* way of contemporary urban living, as featured in the students' discourse and made visible in the film.

School as a social institution has the specific objective of working the historically produced knowledge in/through teaching relations. The film as a cultural production, as a work of art without didactic aims, is a way of poetically dealing with concrete conditions of life. School and film: two spheres of human activity and production become intertwined, affecting and constituting the students' life and development. The school and the *world out there* compose the reality of life. But the film is showing a real, a normal (aspect of) life outside, about which the school keeps silent. So, *normal* at school does not coincide with *normal* in life. The school does not integrate – does not face, analyse, discuss, incorporate – the complex reality of life. And this is also transformed into *normal* conditions of teaching: *déjà dit, déjà vu*.

But in the above situation, the teacher's insistence in asking each student about the consensually admitted *normal* way of living becomes relevant. In the students' voice, *normal* seems to have an acknowledged meaning: "*that's ok, that's the way it is.*" The teacher's persistent questions point to her discomfort and strangeness, possibly suggesting that "it could be different." The intonation here marks positions, distance, and distinctions in the (dis)encounter of voices and experiences.

The tension between "that's the way it is" and "it could be different" acquires visibility in it analysis, as it points to the dynamic heterogeneity of the sign/word and to intrinsic contradictions of the conditions of existence. This tension leads us to inquire about the materiality of signs, the history of meanings, the historicity of signification. This also compels us to reconsider, among other questions, the dialectical means/modes/ conditions of development related to the constitution of personality/ subjectivity.

Overview and Open Questions

In explaining how the environment shapes child development, Vygotsky (1935/1994) proposes an indivisible unit, *perezhivanie*, which implies the individual child in his/her relationships with/in the environment. The notion of *perezhivanie*, integrates emotion (affect, feelings), representation (images), and signification (interpretation, consciousness) in a lived experience. A *same* environment is experienced, *signified* differently by each singular subject. Each subject is affected in a unique manner by the environment.

Vygotsky also called attention to the special role of verbal language in this dynamic interrelationship: "[...] the meaning of children's words is what determines the new relationship which can exist between environment and various developmental processes" (1935/1994, p. 346).

Verbal language is indeed the locus, means, mode, and possibility of the elaboration of consciousness, of the constitution of personality/subjectivity. And here we consider not only what human beings do with signs and words, but what signs and most especially words as human cultural and historical productions do with human beings. If we admit that the sign does not just constitute higher functions, but "the sign changes the interfunctional relationships" (Vygotsky, 1933–34/1997, p. 131), this does not happen in a vacuum.

The analysis of the students' arguing makes visible some aspects of their affective-conceptual elaborations in their comprehension of school and life conditions. Affects and concepts operate in a complicated interrelated system (Vygotsky, 1929/1981). The analysis points to the *drama* lived at the core of interpersonal relationships, where meanings become appropriated – or not (Vygotsky, 1929/1989). We turn our eyes, then, to this *dramatic constitution of human psyche*. Relating empirical situations I and II, we might explore the conditions and the contradictions in such constitutive processes.

Although we configure the social institutional context of school as the locus of our empirical research, the specific contours of a situation lived in this context certainly extend beyond the school boundaries: the cultural historical dimension integrates the concrete material conditions of teaching, learning, and developing. How do material living conditions affect and constitute collective/individual functioning? How does the school mark the students? How does the specific knowledge of such subject-matter have an impact on them?

When the students appropriate – i.e. turn proper, make their own, attempt to understand – geographical concepts and knowledge such as neighborhood, urban space, industry, commerce, etc., they bring to the fore the reality of their lives, which becomes confronted and at the same time intertwined with school knowledge. Within these multiple positions, a new elaboration of concepts, affects, knowledge, and consciousness becomes possible.

How does the film participate in such a process? The students' suggestion indicates the potential of a work of art for knowledge appropriation and consciousness elaboration. The students recognized themselves in the images of the film. They experience a drama of fiction in the reality of their own bodies. The work of art, as a technical-semiotic instrument, as a social technique of sentiment, can be a shared locus of emotional experience. Experiencing contradictory emotions provoked by the work of art mobilizes images, sensations, and feeling that culminate in a *short circuit*, a *cathartic process* (Vygotsky, 1925/1971). This implies an elaborated psychic activity producing *intelligent emotions*. Thinking and emotions are intrinsically intertwined.

But the film at school is not necessarily considered a work of art. It appears as an altered product, with cuts, with a didactic purpose. This way of presenting the film at school provokes different feelings in the students – rage, indignation, revolt. The students who remain for the discussion end up having a space for further and joint elaboration. This moment of discussion is possible due to a history of relationships between the teacher and the students. Although school activities hardly explore the work of art's aesthetic potential, reducing it to moral and pedagogic uses, contradictorily, an opportunity becomes opened for the development of collective awareness, for collective elaboration of concepts and affects, for situating and recognizing distinct social positions.

The film affects students and teacher differently, produces different effects and meanings. Their ways of signifying do not coincide, just as their living conditions and their social positions do not. Social positions make a difference, and they are constitutive of human subjects in interaction with each other. Not only the film but the discussion about the film point to this reality.

When we think about the students' attitudes and interests, which are so often interpreted as far removed from school objectives, we may understand, through this prism, that the whole issue cannot be reduced to a matter of their (lack of) *interest*. Problems cannot simply be characterized as "learning difficulties", or "lack of motivation", as they usually are. In a deeper sense, they concern the issue of different and conflicting expectations, of lack of alternatives in facing the concrete conditions of life; of distant and divergent positions concerning the meanings of knowledge, the meanings of life. This is the *drama* experienced by human subjects in relation to each other at school (cf. Vygotsky, 1929/1989).

We are thus faced with the heterogeneous conditions of the dynamic processes of cultural development, the dramatic constitution of personality, and the equally dramatic features of the relations among teachers and students. In considering the difficult educational reality in Brazilian public schools, as it was shown in this case, we can see how *special* and *normal* become inter-constitutive in the web of social relations: the *normal* way of living appointed by the students is an intrinsic part of the concrete material conditions of their lives and development that define their *special* place at school.

References

Bakhtin, M. (1984). *Ésthétique de la création verbale*. Paris: Gallimard.
Bauman, Z. (2001). *Modernidade líquida*. Rio de Janeiro, Zahar Editores.
Bourdieu, P. (1994). *Raisons pratiques – Sur la théorie de l'action*. Paris: Éditions du Seuil.
Bourdieu, P., Accardo, A., Balzas, G., Beaud, S., Bourdieu, E, Bourgeois, P., Broccolichi, S., Champangne, P. Christin, R., Fagner, J. P., Garcia, S., Lenoir, R. Ouevrard, F.,

Pialoux, M., Pinto, L., Sayad, A., Soulié, C., & Wacquant, L. (1997). *La misère du monde*. Paris: Éditions du Seuil.

Burman, E. (1994). *Deconstructing child psychology*. London: Routledge.

Castells, M. (2004). *The power of identity: The information Age*. Cambridge: Cambridge University Press.

Clot, Y. (1999). *La fonction psychologique du travail*. Paris: PUF.

Danzinger, K. (1990). *Constructing the subject: Historical origins of psychological research*. Cambridge: Cambridge University Press.

Ezpeleta, J. & Rockwell, E. (1986). *Pesquisa participante*. São Paulo: Cortez.

Geertz, C. (1973). *The interpretation of cultures*. New York: Basic Books.

Giddens, A. (1991). *Modernity and self-Identity. Self and society in the late modern age*. Cambridge: Polity.

Góes, M. C. R. de (1992). Os modos de participação do outro no funcionamento do sujeito. *Educação e Sociedade*, 42, 336–341.

Green, J. L., Dixon, C. N., & Zaharlick, A. (2003). Ethnography as a logic of inquiry. In J. Flood, D. Lapp, J. R. Squire & J. M. Jensen (Eds), *Handbook of research on teaching the English language arts* (2nd ed., pp. 201–224). Mahwah, NJ: Lawrence Erlbaum Associates.

Henriques, J., Hollway W., Urwin, C., Venn, C., & Walkerdine, V. (1984). *Changing the subject. Psychology, social regulation and subjectivity*. London: Routledge.

Laplane, A. L. F. de (2000). *Interação e silêncio na sala de aula*. Ijuí: UNIJUÍ.

Nogueira, A. L. H. (1991). *A atividade pedagógica e a apropriação da escrita*. (MA dissertation). Campinas: Faculdade de Educação, UNICAMP <http://www.bibliotecadigital.unicamp.br/document/?code=vtls000033833&fd=y> (date of access: 10/02/2012).

Pino, A. S. (1992). As categorias do público e do privado na análise do processo de internalização. *Educação e Sociedade*, 42, 315–327.

Pino, A. S. (2000). O social e o cultural na obra de Vigotski. *Educação e Sociedade*, 21, 71, 45–78.

Rockwell, E. (1999) Recovering history in the study of schooling: From the *longue durée* to everyday co-construction. *Human Development*, 42, 113–128.

Schneuwly, B. (2002). Le development du concept de development. In Clot, Y. (Ed.), *Avec Vygotski* (pp. 291–304). Paris: La Dispute.

Smolka, A. L. B. (1992). Internalização: Seu significado na dinâmica dialógica. *Educação e Sociedade*, 42, 328–335.

Smolka, A. L. B. (1997). Esboço de uma perspectiva teórico-metodológica no estudo de processos de construção de conhecimento. In Góes, M. C. R. de & Smolka, A. L. B. (Eds) *A Significação nos espaços educacionais* (pp. 29–45). Campinas: Papirus.

Smolka, A. L. B. (2000). O (im)próprio e o (im)pertinente na apropriação das práticas sociais. *Cadernos CEDES*, 50, 26–40.

Volosinov, V., & Bakhtin, M. (1973), *Marxism and the philosophy of language.* (Translated by L. Matejka and I. R. Titunik). New York: Seminar Press. Cambridge, MA: Harvard University Press.

Vygotsky, L. S. (1925/1971). *The psychology of art.* (Translated by Scripta Technica Inc.). Cambridge, MA: MIT Press.

Vygotsky, L. S. (1929/1981). The Genesis of higher mental functions. (Translated by T. Prout and R. van der Veer) In J. V. Wertsch (Ed.), *The Concept of Activity in Soviet Psychology* (pp. 144–188). Armonk, NY: Shape.

Vygotsky, L. S. (1929/1989) Concrete human psychology (Translated by A. A. Puzyrei). *Soviet Psychology*, 27 (2), 53–77.

Vygotsky, L. S. (1933–34/1997). The problem of consciousness (Translated by R. Van der Veer). In Rieber, R. & Wollock, J. (Eds). Problems of the theory and history of psychology. (The collected works of L. S. Vygotsky, Vol 3, pp. 137–138). New York: Plenum.

Vygotsky, L. S. (1934/1987). Thinking and speech (Translated by N. Minick). In Rieber, R. (Ed.), *The collected works of Vygotsky, Vol 1, Problems of general psychology* (pp. 39–288). New York and London: Plenum.

Vygotsky, L. S. (1935/1994). The problem of the environment. (Translated by Theresa Prout and Rene van der Veer) In R. v. d. Veer & J. Valsiner (Eds) *The Vygotsky reader* (pp. 338–354). Oxford and Cambridge: Blackwell.

MARIA JOSÉ R. F. CORACINI

6. The Dis-order of Discourse: Young People Confined in CASA (São Paulo) and a Poet Considered Insane in Colônia Juliano Moreira (Rio de Janeiro)[1]

Every discourse is characterized by an order i.e. social norms and rules that are built to preserve interests and to guide individual behaviors, attitudes, and possible meanings at a certain socio-historical moment. At the same time, this order excludes other meanings, thoughts, and people who, when and if they can, look for singular manners of resisting the power that stems from this order. This paper intends to problematize and discuss the relationship between *order* and *disorder*, between *exclusion* and *inclusion*, as well as between *power* and *resistance*. Such dichotomies cause, in different social situations, interdiction, segregation, and prejudice. The limits and frontiers of such oppositions are however permeable, and should be questioned as to stimulate changes towards a fairer society.

This applies also to the two situations that are studied in this chapter: a confinement imposed by legal authorities and a confinement imposed by the psychiatric establishment. In order to promote the discussion about dis-order, three excerpts written in Brazilian newspapers about "infamous" young offenders living in CASA (Centro de Atendimento Socioeducativo ao Adolescente),[2] in the state of São Paulo, will be presented and discussed. The

1   I am grateful to Ernesto Bertoldo and Carla Tavares, from Universidade Federal de Uberlândia (UFU), in the state of Minas Gerais (Brazil), for having revised this text in English.
2   Center of Social Educational Services for the Adolescent formerly FEBEM (Fundação Estadual para o Bem-Estar do Menor, i.e. State Foundation for the Wellbeing of the Young).

two of them concern the young people' rebellions while the other one tries to defend the rights of these so-called "juvenile delinquents". In addition to this, two oral texts from an "infamous", "black", "poor", and "crazy" woman called Stela do Patrocínio, who lived in a psychiatric hospital asylum in Rio de Janeiro, Colônia Juliano Moreira, for 30 years, will also be examined. In both cases, that of the young people at CASA and of Stela do Patrocínio, custody is a way to discipline and control "docile citizens" so that they obey the established regulation, laws, norms and values. We consider here "delinquency" and "madness" as situations of *marginality* and therefore of *disrespect* for the established order i.e. for the laws that govern every citizen and punish those who violate the legal code of hegemonic society.

For the first case of the young people living in CASA, a broader archive of online and printed newspapers between 1990 and 2000 were examined. It was important for us to understand how Brazilian newspapers spoke about these poor, most commonly previously "homeless" and "addicted to drugs" young people, about their confinement and about the rebellions they took part in. We also analysed how witnesses spoke about them and what the young people said about themselves – if anything.

For the second case, we studied a book entitled *Reino dos Bichos e dos Animais é o Meu Nome* (i.e. *Kingdom of Beasts and Animals is my Name*) by Stela do Patrocínio (2001). Stela do Patrocínio was working as a maid when she had her first "mental crisis" and was then confined in a psychiatric clinic. When she was desperate, she would speak in a loud voice in poems – without rhyme, but with rhythm. These oral poems were tape-recorded by an attendant in the psychiatric clinic and transcribed, after the death of Stela do Patrocínio, by a visitor researcher. After a selection process, a few of those poems were considered good enough to be published.

"Living" in CASA

When writing about the revolts and aggressions committed by "juvenile delinquents" or "young offenders", Brazilian newspapers – on paper or on-line – and magazines of large circulation focus on the competence of policemen in preventing crime and breakout attempts. Less frequent is news of the maltreatment of those young people. The lack of this kind of information in the media may produce the following meaning for the reader: these human beings are "marginal" i.e. "criminal"; they do not deserve pity or defense; they threaten "honest" families and so they must remain in custody, guarded for 24 hours a day. Mothers, by means of non-governmental organizations like the *Association of Adolescents' Mothers (AMA)* or the *Lawyers' Order Association* (an association for the defense of human rights), may speak on the "juvenile delinquents'" behalf. The "juvenile delinquents" have no voice though: other people speak always for them.

Below, we will first examine two brief news stories about a rebellion which took place in 2007. One was written by Cláudio Dias and published on the 1st of May 2008 by the daily newspaper of the Metropolitan region of São Paulo, Brazil, "O Estado de São Paulo":

> On the 3rd of March 2007, a rebellion lasted 15 hours and was characterized by scenes of savagery and throwing computers, a stove, cupboards, and a refrigerator off the roof. This was the most violent action of five rebellions registered in São Paulo State. (translation from Portuguese by the author)

The choice of words: "rebellion", "savagery", "throwing" objects, "violent action", produce the following meaning: the "delinquent" young people are "irrational", and they "respect nothing at all". They destroy even the objects given to them by the authorities, legitimated by the government of the state, the very objects that provide them comfort and maintain the institution intended to recover them, look after them, raise them.

"Mad" and "abnormal", the "offenders'" identities are anonymously built by those who are supposed to be "sane"; these people accuse the juvenile delinquents of being "inconsequent", "thieving" and "criminal"; according to them, the young people make the rebellion just because they are "inconsequent", "thieving" and "criminal". In doing so, they demonstrate that the young people are other-than-humans, without sensitivity or reason; they are exactly where they deserve to be: far away from those who would be in danger if the "violent" and "poor" young people were free. Besides, the quote above mentions the duration of the incident and the number of rebellions that have already happened in São Paulo State. Quantification points to the truth, the information's objectivity i.e. the *systematic* character of the news: the asserted statements in all texts impress their readers with credibility.

Another similar extract is more recent and refers to "rebels" who tried to run away from CASA. This was published on the website "Último Segundo" (Last Second) on the 26th of May 2008 at 19.29:

> Seven young people broke out this afternoon from a Unit of CASA, formerly FEBEM, in Campinas (95 km from São Paulo city). According to the Foundation CASA, six fugitives have been recaptured. The event happened around 14.45. The young people were in the Unity courtyard in São Vicente district for leisure, when at least 15 young people became aggressive towards some employees. Two chaperones charged with promoting leisure activities were injured and quickly taken to a first-aid clinic in the city. Two fugitives stole a car near the Unit, but they have been captured after having lost the control of the vehicle and trying to run away on foot. The Military Police informed that, in the evening, the situation in the CASA Unit was under control. One of the minors who had made the infraction was not recaptured as of nightfall. (Retrieved from <http://ultimosegundo.ig.com.br/brasil/2008/05/26>, 29/7/2008, translation from Portuguese by the author.)

Only the acts of "violence", "insanity", and "criminality" of young people are narrated: their escape, the aggression towards employees, the chaperones who were wounded, and the theft of a car. In direct speech the CASA administration has a voice ("according to CASA ..."), and so does the Military Police ("The Military Police informed ..."). These institutions are responsible for the "order" and punish "disorder": any kind of resistance that corrupts the rules and laws responsible for the safety and well-being of so-called "honest citizens".

"Fugitives" do not have voice. Giving them voice or listening to them would imply admitting that these "insane" and "irrational" young people may have been right in what they did or at least may have had reasons for that. The extract above underlines nothing but the actions of the Military Police and the quick measures taken by CASA, whose goal was to reestablish the "order" and the "law".

The details of the breakout, the way the incident happened, the strict information about locality (Campinas, "95 kilometers away from São Paulo"), time (14.45), and the time of the "fugitives'" capture, as well as the name of the journalist (not copied above), imply recognition, credit and legitimacy. These meanings do not permit questioning the truth of the facts i.e. the objectivity of the journalist who is supposed to (at least explicitly) not utter any kind of judgment. The "juvenile delinquents" are per definitionem positioned within this discursive formation which in turn they try to disorganize as a revenge for their isolation, for the social injustice, for the lack of conditions for a dignified life: a home, a school, health, a job: although they can think, they may not; although they are physically able to speak, their voice is not heard; although they are physically able to see and to hear, they are treated as if they were blind and deaf. According to the order of the hegemonic discourse, they have to accept norms with no question, no protests; they have for example no right to demand what is used or even wasted by rich people. A rebellion seems in this regard to be the only way to speak and be listened to in public: individually the "juvenile delinquents" are almost never heard, seen or taken into consideration. It seems though that they count if not as "citizens", at least as "human beings" from the moment they manifest that they know how to resist.

"There is No Time to Lose"

It is rare that somebody defends "juvenile delinquents" and speaks on their behalf about their problems. The next extract below, presents such a discourse by a lawyer, hired by the Lawyers' Order Association to make a report of what had happened in the facility of CASA:

> Title: There is no time to lose
> Report: In the illuminated courtyard of the Unit of CASA on Imigrantes Road on Saturday night, 11/9, more than one hundred young guys were sitting, wearing only pants, their heads between their knees. Around them, more than ten adults were nervously making rounds. Two men wearing hoods kicked the boys, throwing themselves on the group, trampling on them, in order to attain and spank some of them. Nobody intercepted it. In front of the gates, in the afternoon on Sunday, 12/9, relatives pushed hard against one another and desperately shook the gates. Some minutes before, military policemen made use of guns with rubber balls (which can blind, injure vital

organs, or even kill: who authorized this insane act?) against unprotected parents who wanted to prevent their sons from being led back to CASA. Sometimes the gates are open, ambulances and police cars go in. Mothers ask in vain for information about their sons. (Pinheiro, 1999, online, translation from Portuguese by the author)

In opposition to the previous extracts, which were based on narrations of authorities' testimonies, here the narrator takes the position of an observer in order to report on the event in CASA from within: the focus is on how the "juvenile delinquents" and their families are treated after the rebellion. The report gives all the details to render the scene visually real. But, in spite of the supposed objective information (date, place, time as well as assertive statements, chronological sequence), the extract exposes the perspective of the narrator. Like in a literary text, the narrator brings in his interpretation while trying to defend the victims: The policemen and employees at CASA seem to had "no time to lose" – they needed to proceed very fast in restoring order in the enclosed space. In doing so, they did not hesitate to use all possible measures and aggressive attitudes, with the goal of making the "juvenile delinquents" submit as if they were other-than-humans.

The following day, relatives are also treated badly (they are received with rubber bullets): "after all, how could they intend to defend someone's rights, when he/she does not have any?" They are not given the right as parents to prevent their children from being punished, to know what is happening with their children behind the closed gates in that unit of CASA. Only ambulances and police cars can go in to take care of the injured young people or to punish them. In contrast to the preceding examples, here the narrator takes an explicit position, not only in informing, but also in denunciating: "Nobody intercepted it". The text continues by explicitly defending the young people, listing the maltreatments endured by them (with sticks, with broom handles). Instead of kindness and education, the enclosed young people receive a brutal treatment. The denunciation is strong: behind the narrator's voice the voice of the excluded is heard in indirect speech – as it usually happens when space is given to them who have no voice in the society.

During their rebellions, it is obvious that "juvenile delinquents" can be very "violent", but the "counter-violence" by the Brazilian state is even worse. The Brazilian government has recently taken the decision to build even more shelters that are able to take no more than fifty young people who have committed infractions and compromised the established order. It is supposed that the smaller numbers of "delinquents" will make it easier to enforce vigilance and control. In spite of this, rebellions continue to happen: they are the only way for the young people to be heard, to resist the obscurity, the abandonment, the total disdain of the hegemonic society that wants to see itself out of "danger", "violence", and "insanity".

Post Mortem Poetry by Stela do Patrocínio

Confined to a psychiatric hospital for almost thirty years, far from the judicious eyes of "rational people" i.e. far from the "mentally sane", Stela do Patrocínio suffered. In order to bear the disdain and isolation, she sometimes hid herself behind words that became text – oral, in this case – as a manner of resisting the oppressive system of the psychiatric hospital and surviving the deafness of those who came near to her without paying attention to what she said: the "invalid", "unreasonable" and "discredited" words of a "crazy woman" (cf. Foucault, 1972). "Insane", out of the "rational" parameters of the "sane" or "normal" people, Stela do Patrocínio became an author: she spoke about herself opening her heart, spoke about her hopelessness and her situation of abandonment:

> *In Heaven*
> They told me that God lives in sky
> In sky in land everywhere
> But I don't know if he is inside me
> Or if he is not
> I know that I feel ill in my mouth
> Feeling hungry eating bad
> And feeling ill in my mouth
> Feeding bad eating bad
> Feeling very hungry
> Suffering in my head
> Suffering as a mental patient
> And in the women's prison
> Serving a lifelong imprisonment

Going to court
Going to law
(Patrocínio, 2001, p. 97)[3]

"Crazy" or "lucid"? "Upset" or "deceived"? Maybe neither one nor the other or both? Stela do Patrocínio is conscious of what other people told her before being considered mad (see lines 1–3). She also knows what is happening to her: she has a headache, suffers in her head, "like a mental patient". She feels as if she were in prison ("a lifelong imprisonment") with no hope of one day being free: verbs in gerund ("feeling", "feeding", "eating", "suffering", "serving", "going") and some adjectives ("lifelong") point to something that is happening in an endless time. Like a person who has committed a "crime", a "patient with mental illness", she feels like being in jail. Stela do Patrícínio is "hungry", "hungry" for God, "hungry" for food, lacking everything.

Does Stela do Patrícínio here speak of sensations, of fiction or of truth? One can see here a mixture of all those three elements if one considers that when Stela do Patrícínio speaks for oneself, she *presents* and r*epresents* herself at the same time, like an actor or an actress does in a play:

Days weeks months the entire year
Minute second every hour
Day evening all the night
They want to kill me
They want just to kill me
Because I have an easy life I have a difficult life
They want to know how I can be born
With no facility with difficulty
That's why they want to kill me
(Patrocínio, 2001, p. 64)[4]

---

3   Translation from Portuguese by the author: *No céu:* Me disseram que Deus mora no
     céu/No céu na terra em toda parte/Mas não sei se ele está em mim/Ou se ele não
     está/Eu sei que estou passando mal de boca/Passando muita fome comendo mal/E
     passando mal de boca/Me alimentando mal comendo mal/Passando muita fome/
     Sofrendo da cabeça/Sofrendo como doente mental/E no presidio de mulheres/
     Cumprindo a prisao perpétua/Correndo um processo/Sendo processada.

4   Translation from Portuguese by the author: Dias semanas meses o ano inteiro/Minuto
     Segundo toda hora/Dia tarde noite inteira/Querem me matar/Só querem me matar/

The flux of an endless suffering with no interruption, without limits by chronological time is expressed here. *Me* is juxtaposed to *them*: *me* means life, resistance, force, braveness; *them* refers to the others, the death, the annihilation, the persecution. There is an endless fight: resisting or dying? Choice – if it is possible to choose in such circumstances – is always hard, impossible and possible at the same time ("With no facility with difficulty"). Stela do Patrocínio deconstructs the "logic", the "rationality" of "sane" people and establishes the "logic" of the "poets", of "mad people", of those who succeed in escaping from the monotony of the same and the order. She proceeds as Derrida (1972) explains: by deconstructing the impossible dichotomies and dealing with the "différance" that unifies and, at the same time, separates the oppositions, like the semi-colon does. We argue that these poems represented for the author a singular manner of resisting her suffering, abandonment, misunderstanding, and loneliness. As a kind of catharsis, she opened her heart by confessing her suffering. Her poems are a testimony of a "mentally ill woman"; they reveal injustice; they speak for the silenced people who remain ignored, annulled, and kept out of the social system in contemporary Brazil.

Outlook: From Infamy to Resistance

This chapter, as well as the chapters written by Marcia Aparecida A. Mascia (this volume) and Elzira Yoko Uyeno (this volume), draw on a larger project entitled, "(In-)famous Voices: Discourses of Exclusion and Resistance", which aimed to investigate the discourses of "poor" and "destitute" Brazilian people, including the "homeless" and the "handicapped". Because these people live in the *disorder* or create *another order*, outside of the hegemonic discourse, they are excluded or deleted from social life by those who do not want or cannot even bear to look at them.

Porque eu tenho vida fácil tenho vida difícil/Eles querem saber como é que eu posso ficar nascendo/Sem facilidade com dificuldade/Por isso é que eles querem me matar.

The term *infamous* is taken from Foucault (1977) and means both *unknown* as well as *infamous for having committed a crime* i.e. an act against the hegemonic society.[5] By analysing the discourses about and by such people, we intend to draw attention to an important social and human problem, not only in the academic milieu but, if possible, in broader public domain. We examined here a few texts that speak *for* and *about* the *infamous*, who are simultaneously *not famous at all* and *infamous* because of their resistance; this resistance allowed them to emerge from their anonymity either because of the "violent crimes" they committed or because of the texts they wrote.

There are countless situations of *disorder* and *infamy* in the urban milieu of big Brazilian cities. Unfortunately it is quite common that young people grow in slums, spread over the hills and by the riverside, in big cities, like São Paulo sewing the seeds of fear and of violence while living among the "proper citizens"; it is also typical for Brazil that people die in psychiatric hospitals without any dignity. "Juvenile delinquents" confined in CASA as well as people considered to be "insane" like Stela do Patrocínio are the people whose voices are annulled and have no right to be heard as if there were not "citizens". They grow up in *favelas* or on the street, sooner or later commit some kind of theft or other disturbance of the life of the "honest citizens" and then they are confined in institutions ironically called "CASA" (house, home). There, they continue their other-than-human life, because they are seen as if they do not deserve to live. The human beings, who are born in (or are put into) situations of "risk", are reduced to silence very early, as if their existence was unknown, because what they say has *no meaning*.

In both cases confinement is not a way to solve any problem: According to Derrida (1997), there can be no hospitality if the host imposes his/her norms and values. Hospitality is therefore impossible because a guest is always a "stranger", "different" from the host, while the host does not want to follow "different" ways of life. Hospitality is thus always in-between hostility

---

5   So it happened, according to Foucault (1977), to Pierre Rivière, an insignificant seventeenth-century countryman living in a French village, who planned to hang his mother, sister, and brother in order to save his father from his mother's exploitation.

and hospitality, which Derrida calls *hostipitality*. Indeed the "houses" made for taking care of "juvenile delinquents" and "insane" people, which are in principle built to be *hospitable*, are almost always *hostile* places. The "juvenile delinquents" in CASA are in this sense *at risk*, as is Stela do Patrocínio, whose post mortem poetry speaks for every "mad" person confined to a psychiatric hospital in Brazil. Nobody ever believed in her talent and no one ever thought that, one day, she would become an author, with competence and art.

According to *Novo Aurélio Dictionary*, the word *risk* derives from the Latin *resecare*, which means *to cut*. This definition allows us to say with Abreu (2002) that situations of risk "cut" (i.e. open, widen, create ruptures in) the discourse about "the rights" of "juvenile delinquents" and/or of "psychiatric patients". "Juvenille delinquents" and "mentally ill" people are a "risk" because they say the truths that "good citizens" are unable to utter, censored as they are by reason and culture; they are "mad" because they reveal and disclose what is interdicted; because they do not subordinate themselves to oppressive social norms, and point to an incoherent and instable discourse; because they deconstruct (consciously or not) our normality and unquestionable truths.

In turn, the "good citizens" think they are *at risk* as well because of the "rebellions", the "danger", and the "violence". Foucault (1984, pp. 708–729) refers to resistance as a strategy in consequence of a relation of power: where there is a relation of power, resistance is presupposed. Resistance is important within what Foucault (1971) names the order of discourse (*l'ordre du discours*) because it creates ruptures in it and widens the discourse's incoherencies. "Laws" and "norms", regulated by power relations, constitute the discursive formations that define what can and must be said, which behavior is "acceptable" or not, which values are "legitimated". According to our interpretation, a *discursive formation* means also a *discourse in formation*, i.e. a discourse is never complete, never homogeneous, but always heterogeneous, as well as infinite. Still, if the institutional power legitimates only the knowledge that explains situations of *confinement* as seen from the perspective of the non-confined people, then expressing oneself by means of a rebellion or by means of art seem to be the only way to speak and be listened to in public: it seems that confined "juvenile delinquents" or "psychiatric patients" count if not as "citizens", at least as "human beings" from the moment they manifest that they know how to resist—even if in their effort to penetrate into the hegemonic society, most commonly they crash.

References

Abreu, S. R. de. (2002). Crianças e adolescentes em situações de risco no Brasil. *Revista Brasileira de Psiquiatria*, 24(1), 5–6.

Derrida J. (1972). *Positions*. Paris: Minuit.

Derrida, J. (1997). *De l'hospitalité*. Paris: Calmann-Lévy.

Foucault, M. (1971). *L'Ordre du discours*. Paris: Gallimard.

Foucault, M. (1972). *Histoire de la folie à l'age classique*. Paris: Gallimard.

Foucault, M. (1977). La vie des hommes infâmes. In D. Defert & F. Ewald (Eds) *Dits et ecrits, Vol. 3* (pp. 237–252). Paris: Gallimard.

Foucault, M. (1984). L' éthique du souci de soi comme pratique de la liberté. In D. Defert & F. Ewald (Eds) *Dits et ecrits Vol. 4* (pp. 708–729). Paris: Gallimard.

Mascia, M. A. (this volume). Life at the landfill: Portraying exclusion and resistance in the documentary *Estamira* by Marcos Prado. In: M. Kontopodis, M. C. Magalhães, & M. J. Coracini (Eds), *Facing poverty and marginalization: 50 years of critical research in Brazil*. Oxford: Peter Lang.

Patrocínio, S. (2001). *Reino dos bichos e dos animais é o meu nome*. Rio de Janeiro: Azougue.

Pinheiro, P. S. (1999). FEBEM, humilhação brasileira. *Folha de São Paulo*, 20/09, <http://www.nevusp.org/portugues/index.php?option=com_content&task=view&id=314&Itemid=29> (accessed 28/08/15).

Uyeno, E. Y. (this volume). In-Famous cyberhomelessness: The "homeless" writer Tião Nicomedes. In: M. Kontopodis, M. C. Magalhães, & M. J. Coracini (Eds), *Facing Poverty and Marginalization: Fifty years of Critical Research in Brazil*. Oxford: Peter Lang.

ELZIRA YOKO UYENO

7. In-Famous Cyberhomelessness: The "Homeless" Writer Tião Nicomedes

Following fifteen years of supposedly unrestricted civilian access, the euphoria of claiming that the internet is the latest technological development has ceased. The benefits and losses arising from cyber interaction have divided its interpreters. For those who delight in it, it is a new outer space, containing all of the possibilities of pleasant exploration and progressive change. For others, it is a new outer space containing all of the possible dangers the unknown offers. For sure, the internet is an element of everyday life for most citizens in Brazil while at the same time the discourse of digital inclusion constitutes one of the premises for the success of capitalism in its global phase.

Extending digital inclusion to the doubly "infamous" – the latter being the term used by Foucault (1977) to describe individuals who both do not have fame and committed a vile act – extending it to the "homeless," is such a distant idea that it sounds as ironic as giving "brioche to the people when in lack of bread". Interestingly enough, various media – not only in Brazil but in other parts of the world, too – proclaim that some "homeless" people spend part of their days in cyber cafes. Such claims spark an interest in understanding what kind of use "homeless" people would make of the internet. The subsequent observation that they use it not just for the purpose of having fun, as one might suspect, but rather to participate in social networks, is what triggered this research. Starting from the assumption that cyber interactions can be understood as *simulacrum*, the hypothesis was that "homeless" people participate in social networks under an identity other than that of a '"homeless" person'. Yet, this hypothesis, as we will see below was not verified.

"Homeless" Subjectivity

The cyberhomeless person who is the subject of this article suffers a double exclusion: exclusion from public life that one can call "real", and exclusion from a new public life that is popularly called "virtual" (cf. Kontopodis, Varvantakis & Wulf, 2017). This double allusion necessarily refers to the concept of identity. Identity is an abstract noun, derived from the Latin prefix *ident-icus*, which originally means "the same" from the Latin *idem*, and has been used to denote the set of characteristics and circumstances that distinguish one person or thing, and thanks to which they or it are individualized. The reference "homeless" implies the concept of identity, which, in turn, is linked to subjectivity. Using a "hermeneutics of the subject" as the conducting axis of this complex, intellectual production, it becomes apparent that Foucault's analysis of subjectivation processes presupposes, on the one hand, analysing the socio-historic conditions of objectivity (and therefore the ideological means of exercising power on the subject) and, on the other hand, analysing subjectivity i.e. how the subject is constituted *within* as well as *despite* the given power relations (Revel, 2002). A genealogical concept of power is implied in a great part of Foucault's work, as are biopolitics, which constitutes the means of objectification.

Discipline and Punish: The Birth of the Prison (Foucault, 1975) is written as part of Foucault's genealogical period, during which he was concerned with the social-historical analyses of the submission of the body to confinements in order to observe and discipline the criminals. In his other book *The Birth of the Clinic* (Foucault, 1963), Foucault was worried about the isolation of the sick individual in order to protect the healthy, in spaces controlled by the State. In *Madness and Civilization* (Foucault, 1961), the author analyses the classification of the insane individual according to "psychiatric truth" as socio-historically situated and therefore ideological. These studies led Foucault to claim a relation between *power* and *knowledge*, in the sense that the exertion of *power* over one individual goes together with producing *knowledge* about them.

Complementing Foucault's work, the book *The Abnormal*, published in 2001, was based on a recording of a course taught by Foucault between

1974 and 1975. As Foucault argues, the exclusion of lepers that we now know occurred during the Middle Ages was achieved by a rigorous division between "lepers" and "non-lepers". This led to the constitution of two groups estranged from one another, and finally to the legal and political elimination of the "lepers". The division between "lepers" and "non-lepers" was enforced by rules stating that there was to be no contact between them, that is to say, by the rejection of those by these, by the removal of those beyond the city walls, the community limits.

Foucault (2001) focuses on the rule of leper exclusion outlined since 583 by the councils, which was resumed in 789 by a Charlemagne royal decree, and whose use in the common law grew rapidly in the twelfth and thirteenth centuries. Picking up on further citations of the rule in the statutes of the synods and mentioned in the protocols of church meetings, Foucault (2001, p. 67) describes the ritual of exclusion as similar to a funeral. Around 1400–1430, in the northern and eastern dioceses of France, the leper were subjected to a ceremony of elimination: taken to church with chants of "release me", the leper attended the Mass, as if he were a dead person, hidden under a bier [a tall movable frame on which a coffin is placed] before going through a make-believe burial and being taken to their new dwelling place. These were in fact "practices of *exclusion* and *rejection*" (Foucault, 2001, p. 54) – this is how power is exercised on the "insane", the "ill", the "criminals", the "deviates", and the "poor".

In the documents researched by Foucault on this topic, the mechanisms and the effects of the power exercised on the "different" are described as

> mechanisms and effects of exclusion, elimination, exile, rejection, dispossession, refusal and ignorance; that is the whole list of negative concepts and mechanisms of exclusions. (Foucault, 2001, p. 55)

Note the paradox: the "different" ("deviates", "ill", or "poor") are considered as "equals" in the exercise of power upon them. Continuing Foucault's biopolitical studies, Agamben retells the *homo sacer* condition and explores how exclusion systems are still present under a deceptive appearance. Studying life in classical Greek society, Agamben (1998) states that the Greeks adopted two words to refer to life: *zoé* to refer to the common life of all living beings and *bíos* to refer to the way of living of the individual or a group. Hence *bíos politikós* means political life, and *bios theoretikós*, the contemplative life. The purpose of life – *to zen* – in the polis concerning politics, wrote Aristotle, is more than just living. It is to live a politically active, competent, and therefore respectable life – *to eu zen*. Based on this conception of life, Agamben (1998) studied western politics, rethinking the basis of politics, law, and the political techniques, which created the modern subject. Western politics inserted the modern subject into the city by establishing the rule of law, gradually including natural life in the power of the State, which indicated a shift from *politics* to *bio-politics*. That is to say, introducing *zoé* (natural life) in the *political* field of action by politicizing life.

In this context, the life of a "homeless" person can be seen as the life of a *homo sacer*, which is defined as *destroyable life* or simply *bare life* that does not deserve to be lived. The *homo sacer's* place is always uncertain, excluded from the forensic and political sphere and at the same time framed by it. "Neither political *bíos* nor natural *zoé*, sacred life is the indistinctive zone, in which involving and excluding one another, these are mutually constituted" (Agamben, 1998, p. 98). This creates a complete bare life condition: that which has no place in the forensic and political sphere and is the object of killers. At the same time, instead of searching for a single point from which all forms of power derive, one should rather explore their multiplicity, differences, specificity, and reversibility i.e. study power relationships that intersect with one another to either converge or, on the contrary, oppose and annihilate each other.

Cyber space offers an interesting case of such an intersection of power relations with each other through which power relations sometimes oppose and annihilate each other. Recently developed technologies and the appearance of a virtual public domain have indeed enabled communication technologies to surpass the sender-message-receiver communication model (Sfez, 1993). In the virtual public domain of cyber space, a subject can relate in an imaginary way to oneself and to others, giving up being "what one is". One can be a simulacrum and have a true (secret) identity, and another "cyber identity" in terms of bodies, gender, color, age, social class, etc.

We can ask ourselves, however, if this is possible only in cyber space, since "true" identity can anyway be seen as a result of a socio-historical simulacrum of relations, the result of an imagination that is realized through identifications from the first moment at which an *infant* (the child who still does not speak) is included in symbolic life. Furthermore, according to Pêcheux (1969/1995), the subject, being ideologically determined, has anyway little consciousness about what is enounced and what is "truth". The constitution of the subject as an effect of discourse builds on two illusions: the first is the subject's illusion of being the origin of discourse and the second is the subject's illusion that what one enounces has only one meaning and that everyone understands it in the same way i.e. is the "truth".

In this context, my aim below is to explore how people who, in spite of living in a situation of extreme poverty, resist and perform (not conform with) their identities. This work is part of a broader project called "(In)famous' Voices: Discourses of Exclusion and Resistance" under Maria José Coracini's coordination, and dialogues with her chapter in this book (Coracini, this volume). In order to answer this research question, my analysis focuses on Nicomedes', or Tião's, as he calls himself, diariotiao. zip.net blog because he was the first "homeless" person to create a blog that was well-known among the broader Brazilian public. Tião's posts on his diariotiao.zip.net blog and the material published in the virtual space about him through other resources made up the research corpus. Following a discourse analysis methodology, the chapter examines the socio-historical context within which the discourse on "homelessness" is constructed, before continuing with a micro-analysis of selected texts by cyberhomeless Tião, who lives on the streets in São Paulo and maintains his diariotiao.zip.net blog to this day (accessed for the last time on 5 June 2015).

Tião: The Writer, Blogger and "Homeless" Person

My research data consisted of digital texts posted by Sebastião Nicomedes de Oliveira, or Tião Nicomedes as he is known, since 2007. Tião is a writer and "homeless" person. Although he doesn't mention it in his blog, in his interviews with newspapers and TV programs, he has said he updates the blog from cyber cafes. Sebastião Nicomedes became homeless in 2003, when he was thirty-six years old, after falling from the second floor of a building whilst hanging a sign up on the facade. He ran a "visual communication" store, as he calls it, painting and placing signs on buildings. He had invested all of his money in the business. He was found lying on his left hand, folded like a "Z", his right foot broken and his head crooked. Suspected of having been run over, he was taken to a hospital where he stayed for some time. Discharged from hospital without any calls from Simone, who he called his fiancée, broke, with his arm plastered up to his shoulder, he went to sleep on the streets near "Mercadão" (the market) where he could eat leftover of fruits and vegetables. He later asked for shelter at a hostel. Nothing was left from his store: saying that Tião was dead, his employees had sold the machinery and returned the property to the owner. He lost his parents early in his life and was raised by his grandmother.

He started living with his sister but, due to the embarrassment of the financial difficulties he caused her as she and her husband raised their children, he decided to lead a wandering life: from hostels and shelters he ended up on the streets. This was how Tião joined the "homeless" community – those whose identities (con-)form the (in)visible: invisible because we deviate our gaze away from them, because they annoy us; visible because they occupy the public space, because they are placed between those who pass through. In this scenario, several times described by Tião in his works – "Lazy Bonifacil"; "Aline, Simone and other bad girls" a book of poems; "Diary of a cart-driver", a monologue; and lately, "A man with no country", a play he staged in alternative theaters – the menace of death always exists. Interestingly enough though, Tião Nicomedes participated in founding the National Movement of the Homeless Population in Brazil a few years later, engaging in various forms of activism to support "homeless" people – reinventing his condition as a *homo sacer* not only "online" but also "offline".

A Different Easter ...

I would like to introduce Tião Nicomedes's writing style by presenting a text from his blog <bloguedotiaozipnet.com.br> (translated from Portuguese by myself):

EASTER TIME
This has been a different Easter! Once again
I spent Holy Saturday, and Easter Sunday, by myself.
Next holidays, I want to see my family, and to get myself a nice girlfriend.
To have more friends who would have me in their homes.
Because this label of homeless has been an obstacle!
There are some people I have known for years, but they never invite me for a cup
of coffee.
That's the difference, that's what made this Easter so special [...]

As his blog diariotiao.zip.net explains, this text follows a diary structure: the post or diary entry above refers to the Easter Sunday of 2007. Tião opens his diary entry with the utterance "a different Easter!" using an exclamation mark that semantically retains a positive meaning. Upon a first reading, what comes next: "Once again/I spent Holy Saturday by myself" might sound strange to the reader as it does not meet the expectation of its opening. The expression "Once again", although in the same line as "This has been a different Easter!", refers to the next line – that he spent Holy Saturday and Easter Sunday all alone. Analysing this passage, we will see that he thinks that these dates should be celebrated with family or friends, and that this belongs to another life, the life of an "included", as it is followed by: "Next holidays, I want to see my family, and to get myself a nice girlfriend. To have more friends who would have me in their homes".

What starts as a "description" of the day turns into a reflection about his present "homeless" condition: "Because this label of homeless has been such an obstacle!" Tião uses the word *label* to refer to the "homeless", a term that indicates an attributed identity. In "it has been such an obstacle", the verb tense *has been* shows an action in process, which is, therefore, a continuous perception of obstacles that the "homeless" label has brought him. "There are some people I have known for years, but they never invite me for a cup of coffee" says that the "homeless" identity is socio-historically built on exclusion: people with whom he used to relate when he was an included member of society now segregate him, as was historically the case for the leper.

In a slightly different mode but in the same frame, the next part describes the lives of "homeless" people who occupied an abandoned building in São Paulo city:

I decided to go for a walk and send away monotony. I went after those who respect me:
The homeless people. I went to check out Luz's new occupation
The just-occupied building on Mauá street.
Among the homeless, I am always welcome!!
Whole families, humble people, kind people, good-hearted people!!
Going up the stairs, I saw kids playing around,
Teenagers flirting, young people listening to music, beautiful youth!
Some electricians fixing things, changing bulbs.
On the fourth floor, I ran into some tough women
Doing their laundry on Easter Sunday!
I asked: Is it Easter? And I heard back: Happy Easter, Tião.
The shining eyes, the smiles, the happiness.

The (dis-)similarity of his "homeless" condition stands out when Tião refers to this condition as different from that of those who live on the streets, but as different to those in the included position who segregate him. "I went after those who respect me: the homeless people. ... Among the homeless I am always welcome!" Tião refers to the "homeless" people affectionately: "Whole families, humble people, kind people!" Tião does not refer to all of the various "homeless" people he may meet on the streets. He writes that he had gone to "check out Luz's new occupation – the just-occupied building on Mauá street", mentioning a central region in São Paulo and an abandoned building that had been taken as housing by a group of "homeless" people.

After making references to feeling *welcome* by them, Tião starts describing those people's lives, recalling the feelings he had been taken by: going up the stairs he saw kids playing, teenagers flirting, young people listening to music, men at work; on the fourth floor, he ran into some women doing their laundry as if it were an ordinary day. We realize that the importance Tião attaches to Easter Sunday is part of his "other life" when he asks: "Is it Easter? Happy Easter, Tião", a woman replies, demonstrating that someone in the group knows him, perhaps a former "homeless" person who lived on the street (now a "homeless" person living in the old building). Instead of hearing complaints about working during Easter, Tião sees "shining eyes, the smiles, the happiness".

You know, I have lived on the streets, in shelters, and temporary homes.
What's the difference between the homeless and the people of the street?
But there is not much union, there is not much proximity and respect.

> Capitalism does it, it divides people, makes trouble.
> Capitalism is going to cause the end of days soon.
> We have to stop this thing of hatred among the poor
> We have got to get together and stand up for ourselves.
> Twelve thousand homeless people.
> Three million people under the poverty line [...]

As the poem continues, one can see the hybrid dimension of Tião's text: if up to that point it was an ordinary diary, some traits of virtual writing set in when interacting with the virtual reader: "You know, I have lived on the streets, in shelters, and temporary homes". He seems to be sharing with the reader. Having shared his situation as a "homeless" person, the blog writing offers traits of confession as described by Foucault: by speaking of himself to someone else, Tião appears to gain an understanding of his condition. This comprehension happens first when Tião bonds with the "homeless" people (i.e. his inclusion in this class, as the Lacanian proletariat postulation), in order to, then, using this bond, position himself in the broader context of the contemporary "capitalist" world (in his words).

When he writes "What is the difference between the homeless and the people of the street?", Tião seems to realize the similarity between the two in terms of exclusion. He then recognizes a certain lack of class consciousness when he writes "but there is not much union, there is not much proximity and respect". The first movement, bonding with the excluded class, appears to take place when he uses "we" instead of "I", without explaining the ambiguity: "We have to stop this thing of hatred among the poor". Then, his text moves away from being a diary and a blog, acquiring the structure of a manifesto ("We have got to get together and stand up for ourselves ..."). Here he denies his condition as he did at the beginning of the text when he said that he resented the effects of being labeled "homeless". This positioning gives Tião and his peers an identity: Tião's "subjective transformation", as Zizek (2007) stipulates, happens in the reflexive moment of the declaration and not at the moment of action:

> They lost government aid, but they were not out on the street.
> Then, I understood and thought: GOD, that's it!
> These people want to work, to have somewhere of their own, and to live in peace.

This excerpt shows us Tião's conclusion about the women who do their laundry on an Easter Sunday and who smile and wish him a "Happy Easter", despite having lost their government aid. They didn't end up on the streets. Instead, they occupied an empty real estate and moved on with their lives. Considering that Tião posted this text after visiting them, his perception happened at the time of typing his post and not at the time of his visit. As Zizek (2007) argues, this reflexive communication implies that a statement does not only transmit some content but, simultaneously, transmits the way in which the subject relates to that statement.

Final Considerations

The "homeless" people are (in-)famous, with the particularity of not necessarily having committed a vile act that would remove their anonymity. Their "villainy" instead rests on not having a "fixed" residence, a basic condition for doing justice to the defendant using *in dubio pro reo* and *habeas corpus*, principles that are significant for justice and for democracy. This is the socio-historical, therefore, ideological "homeless" condition. This villainy defines the "homeless" person as a contemporary *homo sacer*: placed simultaneously *inside* and *outside* the legal and political system, the "homeless" person becomes one whose life or death is irrelevant. Although the "homeless" person has the civil right of having her/his physical integrity preserved, her/his life is subject to attacks that have often not been considered crimes. Not considering them as crimes denounces justice in form not in substance: the cry of the "homeless" person is just noise, not a voice, since it is uttered by the powerless. It is a "misunderstanding" in the sense imputed by Rancière (1995) that the words "civil rights" have different meanings for the "homeless" and for the institutions that should preserve their rights.

It is therefore possible to postulate that "homeless" people are the (in-)famous – the parentheses giving them both fame and no fame. They are *invisible* not because they are imperceptible, but due to the deviation of the other peoples' eyes to avoid seeing them. Their fame is exploited by the media when they fall victim to vile acts, from deviated looks to cowardly killings, ranging from being the target of liquid waste, to calling them names, being evicted and suffering physical assaults. This socio-historically, and therefore ideologically produced disgrace pre-disposes them to subsequent occurrences that turn them into a contemporary *homo sacer*, whose life is a "destroyable life" (cf. Agamben, 1998).

It is due to these historical circumstances of exclusion that providing "homeless" people with digital inclusion is like giving them brioche. In times of a *modus vivendi* determined by the hegemonic discourse of cybernetics, the "homelessness" extends the term *(in-)famous*. As the "homeless" person is the *homo sacer* of public space, cyberspace throws another perverse exclusion on the "homeless": they become excluded from the virtual space too. Thus, the "homeless" person becomes doubly *(in-)famous*, and a double *homo sacer*. The "homeless" constitute the perfect prejudged subjects.

Yet, Tião Nicomedes's virtual prose has a symbolic function, whose performative dimension exceeds that of Austin and Searle: it achieves a "double movement", i.e. being transposed to the reality of being "homeless" as well as a blogger, Tião defends his class from the exclusion systems, from the infamy and from the *homo sacer* condition. Being included in the class of cybernauts was the first forthcoming movement. The second was to expose, on this new public virtual space, the *homo sacer* condition of his peers. We can also see that every statement not only transmits some content, but also simultaneously transmits the way a person relates to this content, as Zizek (2007) recognized. This double movement seems to constitute part of Tião's identity-building. It permitted him to reinvent himself. It also allowed him to become responsible for his life, including the parts of it that are contingent to him. Tião does not accept the socio-historical dynamics of contemporary life, and therefore does not conform. He performs to the ethics of desire, in the sense of leading his life according to what is most dear to him.

References

Agamben, G. (1998). *Homo sacer: Sovereign power and bare life.* Stanford: Stanford University Press.

Certeau, M. de (1990). *L'invention du quotidian: L'arts de faire.* Paris: Gallimard.

Coracini, M. J. (this volume). The Dis-order of discourse: Young people confined in CASA (São Paulo) and a poet considered insane in Colônia Juliano Moreira (Rio de Janeiro). In: M. Kontopodis, M. C. Magalhães, & M. J. Coracini (Eds), *Facing Poverty and Marginalization: Fifty Years of Critical Research in Brazil*. Oxford: Peter Lang.

Foucault, M. (1961). *Folie et déraison. Histoire de la folie à l'age classique*. Paris: Plon.

Foucault, M. (1963). *Naissance de la clinique. Une archéologie du regard médical*. Paris: Presses Universitaires de France.

Foucault, M. (1976). *Histoire de la sexualité I. La volonté de savoir*. Paris: Gallimard.

Foucault, M. (1977). La vie des hommes infâmes. *Les Cahiers du Chemin*, 29, 12–29.

Foucault, M. (2001). *L'hermeneutique du sujet*. Paris: Éditions du Seuil.

Kontopodis, M., Varvantakis, C., & Wulf, C. (Eds) (2017). *Global youth in digital trajectories*. London: Routledge.

Pêcheux, M. (1969/1995). Automatic discourse analysis. In: Hak, T. & Helsloot, N. (Eds). *Automatic discourse analysis* (pp. 63–122). Amsterdam/Atlanta, GA: Rodopi.

Rancière, J. (1995). *La mésentente*. Paris: Galilée.

Revel, J. (2002). *Le vocabulaire de Foucault*. Paris: Ellipses Édition.

Sfez, L. (1993). *Critique de la communication*. Paris: Seuil.

Zizek, S. (2007). *How to read Lacan*. New York: WW Norton.

MICHALIS KONTOPODIS

Instead of an Epilogue. Youth "in Movement" in Contemporary Brazil: Sharing Intense Moments with José, Carlos, Raquel, and Werá Mirim

This ethnographic narration aims to conclude the volume "Facing Poverty and Marginalization" by taking the reader into various youth worlds emerging in today's Brazil. The focus refers to young men and women whose everyday lives are currently changing within the context of broader social and political movements. Four scenes of particular emotional intensity are presented. I use these scenes to refer to broader observations about a few of Brazil's most significant ongoing urban and rural social movements presented in the previous chapters (the Landless Rural Workers' movement, indigenous movements, movements for the education of urban workers and/or "homeless", and the National Movement of the Struggle for Housing). My narration is based on observations I made during an ethnographic field research of several months at different places of Brazil in collaboration with local colleagues in 2010 and then again in 2013. These ethnographic observations would not have been possible or accurate without the help and participation as well as the hospitality of many Brazilian colleagues (see acknowledgements) who have been in the various research fields for longer, enabled my access there, and provided me with further data and their views to ensure the validity of my observations.

In response to the arguments presented in the previous chapters, I will briefly explore how these movements conceive youth and education. I will also search for subcultural elements in the everyday lives of the observed young people and highlight modes of resistance to capitalist forms of work and living that have recently emerged in the Brazilian periphery. I will use experimental ethnographic writing and literature techniques in order to share complex sensorial, emotional, and meaning-related experiences and imaginations. The methodology of my study follows post-1986 ethnographic approaches (cf. Emerson, Fretz, & Shaw, 2003; Faubion & Marcus, 2009; Marcus, 1986, 1998) with a specific focus on youth, resistance, and Otherness (cf. Friebertshäuser, 2003; Hall & Jefferson, 1976). My work is especially inspired by recent discussions in the anthropology of emotions (Tonkin, 2010; Wulf & Gebauer, 2010). It is also inspired by the experimental ethnographic writing of M. Taussig (2004, 2006) and experiments with the role that emotions and remembering/forgetting play in research as well as in writing.

José at Escola Porto Alegre

José[1] is there again, as usual poorly dressed. He looks up for a moment when I enter, then returns to his work. His patience has always been remarkable to me. Now again I observe him standing, his whole body turned to the desk, as his hands, gently or firmly as necessary, glide across the pieces of paper, glue, metal cords, scissors, dried leaves, and other materials he works with. I can see his face only if he needs something from another desk, when he turns to look for it. He then moves quickly but lightly across the wooden floor, searches through a drawer, and takes what he needs; he does so without looking to me or the others in the room, quickly returning to his work.

José is there almost every day – the work has now progressed, and notebooks with nicely decorated hardcovers have been produced. Marcia, the teacher, remains invisible for most of the time, but she sometimes might help for a moment or two, commenting on or arranging the newly made notebooks. The room is not very well-lit and everything there is old – tables, cupboards, desks, chairs. Even the walls should have been painted a long time ago. Quite a lot of tools and some machinery (to cut or press paper etc.) are lying around, but there is no particular decoration. I look out of the window

---

1   All names in the chapter are pseudonyms in order to protect anonymity. For the same reason, no detailed information is given about the concrete places or/and period in which this research took place, and age-related information is approximate.

to the schoolyard – although there is a break now, not many students are around. The school's general assembly, where students and teachers have an equal vote, begins after the break at 9.00 – in a few minutes. José is not going – he prefers to work with paper in the school's paper-working room. I am impressed how well he deals with all the tools and materials and like his products very much – hardcovers for books and notebooks in all possible shapes and colors, decorated with ink drawings and dried flowers.

Arts constitute one of the most important subjects at this school, which is based on the principles of communitarian therapy (Barreto, 2005; Ferreira-Filha & Dias, 2006) and Freireian pedagogy (Freire, 1986). José still has to learn mathematics, Portuguese, and history as well as computers, environmental and political education, and other subjects that are decided by the general assembly and taught in thematic project mode. He is a 16-year-old student. Similarly to all other students – who are between 13 and 24 years old – José is offered a basic level of education that correlates more to what in other contexts would be primary school knowledge. About 100 students are registered, and half of them participate regularly.

The school, where we are, is a quite well known school for "homeless" students in Porto Alegre, Brazil: the Escola Porto Alegre (EPA). The Escola Porto Alegre emerged in the context of *educação popular* – a broader Brazilian movement for public education for all.[2] This school is in many regards an *open* school (escola aberta): it is first of all *open* in the sense that a student is *welcome* at the school, but is not *obliged* to stay there;[3] the school is also in many regards *open* for students who would elsewhere feel marginalized; it is *open* for the residents of the school's neighborhood during the afternoon; it is *open* in the sense of its direct participation in the city's councils as well its collaborations with many other institutions – even international ones.

---

2   For general information on the Brazilian educational scape in English see Kontopodis, 2009.

3   This *openness* is quite an unusual condition for Europeans. It goes together with another idea: that a student is eligible to graduate the school not after a certain number of school years, but whenever the teachers assess that the student has successfully accomplished his/her school education, independent of what day or month it is.

Furthermore, the school has since the very beginning (1995) been *open* to all possible changes on all levels – which have been suggested, discussed, and decided by a general assembly in which all interested students and all teachers participate. I was impressed to realize that the teachers were very well read and were knowledgeable about a wide range of subjects, from Foucault and Deleuze & Guatarri to contemporary Brazilian educational research and discussions, e.g. about ethnomathematics or teacher education. Although more schools of this type were established in Porto Alegre some years ago, this is the only school that has kept this *openness* at all levels – all other similar schools have retreated to less *open* – or radical – modes of organization.

The school does, however, close during the night (for both students and teachers), and although there is a general assembly with an equal participation of teachers and students, the teachers are the ones who permanently work there and constitute the "core" or the "heart" of the school. When all classes have finished for the day, students are still allowed to remain at the school until seven p.m. to work at the various laboratories with ceramics or paper. Then the school closes.

Where José slept the night before is an open question: according to his teachers and his own narrations, he does not have a family, he does not have a home, and he does not currently belong to a certain gang or some other group that would provide him with food and security. When the school doors open for students, he goes quickly through the schoolyard to the rooms at the right to take a shower. How good it is that there is always hot water, and one can even wash one's clothes at school! This is one of the very few places where José can take a shower. It is also one of the very few places – if not the only one – where José can have breakfast: bread, butter, marmalade, and coffee. This is served to all students for free and paid by the municipality of Porto Alegre (as is also the case with lunch and snacks several times through the day).

José has just received the amount of 50 Reais for the notebooks he sold through the school last month. He must still collect cans and other recyclable materials from the streets and sell them to supplement his income. I am not sure what his expenses are. He does not have a home and cannot afford a mobile phone; he gets food at the school, as well as some used clothes or other things that might be donated to the school from the neighborhood.

Drug-dealing for male students and prostitution for the female ones are quite common activities among the students of this school – but not for José, who is very enthusiastic about the paper cover construction and is slowly creating a network of clients for his paper products. Perhaps some day he will earn his whole living with it.

Soon it will be night, the school (home?) will be closed again, the night will begin and the night is hard. I continue to observe how he cuts the paper, he looks like so concentrated, intense moments of silence pass by ...

Carlos at a Settlement of the Landless Rural Workers' Movement at Espírito Santo

Carlos, Carlos's father, and I sit inside their home speaking about nothing in particular. We have eaten well – as usual self-produced chicken, rice, and then fruit juice – and we layback quite lazy. It is hot, we are all dressed simply and lightly: shorts, T-shirts, slippers. One would not say that any of us made any particular effort to combine colors or styles. It is about three p.m., there is no work to do – neither in the fields nor for the school, because it is summertime. Carlos's 7-year-old sister wants my attention and walks around inventing a series of plays. I give her my video recorder to play with; she laughs happily and disappears outside the home.

I observe the huge flat screen TV of the family, which I have seen in every home I have been in Brazil – in intellectuals' apartments, *favelas*, or Guarani Indians' wooden houses. There is a TV table, quite luxurious, with extra space for a CD player and speakers that also look new and fancy. The sofa reminds me of the sofa in my middle-class parents' living room. For a moment I forget where I am. But then the posters hanging on the wall behind the sofa, opposite the TV, draw my attention. They depict historical moments of the Landless Workers' fights.

As explained in the chapter of this volume by Isabela Camini & Michalis Kontopodis (this volume) the Landless Rural Worker's Movement in Brazil ("Movimento dos Trabalhadores Rurais Sem Terra,") is considered the major counter-hegemonic movement of Brazil and one of the most important radical social movements of Latin America, with an estimated 1.5 million landless members of all possible ages and ethnic-racial groups organized all over Brazil.[4] The settlement where I am was founded 15 years ago, and trees are now big enough to produce enough fruit for the whole year. It is one of the richest and most vibrant settlements of the Landless Movement.

I remember my talk yesterday with Carlos, the son:

> "Are you going to come back to the settlement after your studies?"
> "I don't know what I will think in such a moment after a few years, but I guess yes."
> "It is good to travel when you are young – like I am doing now – and also to live in a city for a few years but in the long term I also want to return to the island where I was born."
> "Yes, I do not like cities," Carlos said laughing;
> "Neither do I."
>
> (translated from Portuguese by the author)

The formerly illiterate and marginalized urban or rural populations who made up the Landless Workers' Movement in the very beginning occupied lands they intended to cultivate in an ecological and direct-democratic way, but this was not all: they also occupied nearby universities and founded schools as well as training programs for people from the movement to become teachers in these schools inside the settlements (da Silva, 2008; de Andrade, 2008; Farias, 2008). A series of such programs and institutions allowing Landless Workers to become teachers at the landless schools have been established – often in cooperation with local universities (Diniz-Pereira, 2005; Foerste, 2004, 2009).

Carlos is now 17 years old. He received his primary education at a public (i.e. state funded) school inside the settlement, which was constructed and

---

4   For general information about the Landless Worker's Movement, its history and political and educational aspirations in English, see Camini & Kontopodis, this volume. Pizetta & Souza (2005) offer a detailed presentation in Portuguese of the history of the Landless Worker's Movement at Espírito Santo, in particular, in its different phases: its first steps from 1983–1985; the constitution of the movement at Espírito Santo, 1985–1988; further conflicts and repression from 1989–1991; new fights from 1992–1994: the establishment and expansion of the movement, 1995–2002: and the Landless Movement under the Lula government at Espírito Santo from 2003–2005. The scene presented here took place in 2010 and explores developments that follow the history presented by Pizetta & Souza.

administered by the Landless Workers' Movement. He then started his secondary education at a school in the nearby town, because there was no secondary school inside the settlement. The secondary school he attends is semi-public – common enough for the region –and run by the Jesuit church. It applies a specific pedagogy called *pedagogia da alternancia* (pedagogy of alternation, cf. Ribeiro, 2008). In one year Carlos is quite sure that he will get a place at the region's university to study agricultural science. The father speaks about Carlos's plans. Carlos listens, laughs, but lets his father explain everything. He then rests back for while, daydreaming. I observe for a moment Carlos's father's smiling face – a smile that somehow reflects both pride and serenity.

Carlos has just received a guest – a young girl from the settlement, whom I have already seen a few times here and there. In a very simple way, slowly, but neither secretly nor loudly, they leave for a walk. "Where did Carlos go?" "They always meet around this time," says his father, not exactly answering my question. Fernanda, the daughter, is now in front of the house, feeding a few chickens moving about the yard.

After a while Carlos's father says that he will show me the pump, responding to my interest in learning more about the settlement's employment of agricultural technologies. We move in the direction of his motorbike, he gets on and waits for me to take my video camera and whatever else I think I might need. We are on what can be seen as the "main road" of the settlement, connecting the district where people live with the school and the various fields where people work. We pass in front of the school; then again I see a few houses with small yards built here and there. I note that there is no "central" square, meeting place as in European villages. The place somehow most "central" and "public" is the school – where indeed sometimes all the residents meet to discuss common issues. In front of the school there is a provisory football ground, though it is not much used by the adult residents.

I know that we will soon pass by quite a large lake – it is artificial, but old enough to fit well into the landscape consisting of hills in the background and green fields all around us. Just a few seconds before I can see the lake I catch sight of Carlos and his young girlfriend sitting on a rock at the right, as if they have been there for hours and hours. They do not move and are silent, just enjoying the view of the lake, both intently studying the landscape.

Fig. 5: The lake that Carlos and his young girlfriend were watching
(copy of the original photograph taken by the author – courtesy of Carlos' father)

The road passes between them and the lake, we pass in front of them, nobody seems surprised, nobody moves, nobody is disturbed. It seems self-evident how things are, and it seems self-evident that we do not stop to say hello. I look for a moment at Carlos's face, he is tranquilly smiling.

Raquel at an Occupied Housing Project of the National Movement of the Struggle for Housing (MNLM) in Porto Alegre

It is morning and I arrive at the occupied housing project where Raquel lives – a young woman of about 20 years old. She is waiting for me with a smiling face and her one-and-a-half-year-old daughter in her arms. Today the whole house has a lot to do – a celebration is going to be organized for coming Saturday, with many activities: live music, film projections, a theatre-play for the kids, etc. Raquel stays with me for a moment and then tries to coordinate everything and runs all over the place.

I talk a little bit with Newton, another young resident, and he explains to me how important the support of the broader local community is for their housing project. They need a lot of support now, especially in fighting against the police's violence, which has recently been on the rise: the municipality wants to take over the place as well as a nearby *favela* and construct entertainment spaces for tourists to use on the occasion of the 2014 Porto Alegre football cup. The forthcoming party should contribute to getting such support, inform people about the movement, and create further networks of solidarity.

To prepare everything and make a good impression to the broader local community during the party implies a lot of work, but everybody seems enthusiastic about the whole event and keen on participating in all tasks. The atmosphere is great. Raquel seems to be the most enthusiastic of all – and everybody seems to trust her in her coordinating role. Like most people here, she moved to this occupation about a year ago. Before she was living in a *favela* with her husband, baby, and other people. They did not have enough space for their "new" family, so they moved out.

We begin to clean the place – at the same time some people open the doors of the backyard and deal with the many people who come to park their car there for the whole day. This is one of the main financial resources of the families living in this occupied space, although they also sell T-shirts and organize parties. In this way they manage somehow to cover their expenses for food, clothes, phone and internet (they do not pay for electricity or water but just take them directly from the public electricity and water network).

Raquel does not have much time to help with everything, because at 12.00 she is going to go to school – another school established in the context of public education for all (*educação popular*). The CMET, municipal center for the education of workers (Centro Municipal de Educação dos Trabalhadores), is a huge school in a small building that works on three shifts: 8h–12h; 14h–18h; 18h30–22h30. Raquel attends this school voluntarily and is offered basic, i.e. primary, education there. CMET shares some similarities to Escola Porto Alegre but is bigger and addressed – as its name reveals – to workers of all possible ages, not only to young people. It has a lot of students with special needs (about 1/5), groups of students of all ages, and about 86 teachers and 1,000 students in total. Most of the students are 18–36 years old, although the age may vary from 15 to 88 years. Arts – and especially theater – play a central role in the curriculum here, and absences count only for students who are less than 18 years old. CMET is organized on the principles of solidarity, civil engagement, and moral autonomy. Raquel feels welcome and respected there – which is the reason why she does not attend any other school, as she explains to me.

It is time for a brief coffee break. We go to the large common room of the occupied space. Raquel holds a piece of paper with notes, and soon begins to summarize everything that should be done to everybody from the 23 families living there, and who is responsible for what: decorating, buying and transporting drinks, cooking, setting up the sound system, photocopying fliers etc. I pay attention once again to the graffiti drawn all over the place, as well as to the posters announcing various political events. Somehow this background fits well with the rather punk appearance of most of the people here: jeans with holes, punk red-and-green haircuts, rings, tattoos, red-and-black T-shirts advertising the *Movimento Nacional pela Luta pela Moradia* (MNLM) i.e. National Movement of the Struggle for Housing – also known as National Movement of Housing Vindication.[5] "While being a resident is a privilege, occupying is a right" is written on the wall – the main motto of this young Brazilian movement, which some people consider to be the urban version of the Landless Rural Workers' Movement.

Everybody pays attention to what Raquel is saying. I like her calmness, optimism, and engagement. She smiles all the time, responds to all questions calmly, and also cares for her baby whom she is carrying, playing with it now and then. I enjoy the scene and remember similar meetings that I have experienced in quite different occupied spaces in Greece and in Germany, where I lived a few years ago.

---

5   For a broader analysis and information on this movement in English, see Comerlato, Stumpf Buaes & Pólvora, this volume.

Fig. 6: Large common room of occupied territory by the Movimento Nacional pela
Luta pela Moradia (National Movement of the Struggle for Housing)
(photographed by the author)

Werá Mirim in a Guarani Community

It is morning – but I do not have a feeling that time matters in any way. I
sit in a circle with Werá Mirim[6] and a few other young men around 16 years

6   Guarani people were prohibited from using officially their Guarani names and language
during the Brazilian dictatorship – so they often had two names, one for them, one for
the state. Guarani was also prohibited as a language in schools. Although this practice
continued until the '80s, even nowadays they usually have a non-Guarani name and a
Guarani one, and they use the different names in different contexts (depending on the
presence of non-Guarani people and other factors). I asked the young people whom
I associated with for their Guarani names and chose to use here a Guarani name as a
pseudonym as a gesture of respect to the Guarani culture and language. This name is
commonly used for Guarani men and means something like "young sacred person".

old on the floor in front of their home (a construction made out of wood and soil, with a metal roof so that the rain water does not enter). Werá Mirim holds a guitar and a notebook with handwritten verses and notes. He laughs, tries to play and sing one of the songs – but as he says, he does not know anything, and cannot play well at all. He is not practicing, just playing here and there, letting time pass by. The music is not Guarani; it is Brazilian and Latin American pop. The spoken language is Portuguese – with a particular dialect and some words in Guarani, which I do not understand. Even more meaningful than spoken language is silence, which includes "listening" to each other being silent.

The guitar is passed around and the other young men play as well, until it comes back to Werá Mirim. They also laugh, trying to play and sing one of the songs – but they all say that they do not know how to play anything well, and are just letting time pass by. I encourage them to sing and play other songs, songs they haven't yet tried – they laugh. Time passes by; Werá Mirim is now playing again. It seems to me that the same scene goes on forever and ever. Everybody is relaxed, there is nothing in particular to do or to talk about, it is not too hot, other residents move around and pass by, as do some chickens and a dog, but my feeling is that nothing moves – not even time ... The young men do not seem to care about anything in this concrete moment. Playing the guitar continues, with small talk in-between, they are now laughing because Werá Mirim has sung a funny song in a strange way. At some point two of the young men disappear – they have gone to pee in the forest instead of using the toilets built by the state a few years ago, which look quite nasty.

I know that some other young men – among them Werá Mirim's brother – moved to nearby cities a year ago, while a few years back a whole group of the village residents – including Werá Mirim's biological father – moved to another forest that was supposedly more bountiful in water, plants and food. Werá Mirim has not seen them since then, but this seems

---

The spoken language is *português índio* – with a particular dialect and some words, and structures in Guarani, which I do not always understand. For further details on the issue of multilingualism, see Rodrigues Mendes, this volume.

to be quite normal – he only spoke about it because I asked. At what can be considered a "central square" – two minutes away from the place we sit – an assembly is going on to discuss issues regarding identity politics and the maintenance of Guarani culture. The young people with whom I am do not seem interested or obliged in any way to participate. It seems that whatever could be a "present problem" or a "future aim" – pursuing one's luck in a city just out of curiosity, moving to another countryside place because of a lack of resources, or being threatened by the culture of "white men," as the cacique, the oldest person in the village, would say – is far away. There is no need to think about those things or actively do anything else than sit in a circle and play the guitar.

One could expect these youngsters to go to the public (i.e. state-funded) school, which was built within walking distance by the Brazilian state and opens just for them, but they are not very interested. The cacique, the oldest person in the settlement, would expect them to participate in various rituals that take place in a Guarani church – but rituals take place mainly during the evening and night and the village does not yet have a Guarani church anyway (cf. Tangerino, 1996).

I look at Werá Mirim and observe his mohawk. I think of the cacique who strongly criticizes "his" young people for not accepting his principles and being under the influence of the "white man's" fashion, adopting hair-styles and appearances that are not Guarani. At the same time, it is very clear to me that no young white people would have the style Werá Mirim has. Although it might be a "new trend" among the Guaranis, it is "Guarani" – not *traditional* Guarani, but *subcultural* Guarani. However, it still marks the Guarani young men's Otherness to most of their peers who live in the nearby villages and cities.

Playing the guitar goes on in the way I described above. It might have been two hours that we have been here, we are relaxed; other residents – also chickens and the dog – move around or pass by but we do not react in any way. Werá Mirim holds the guitar and the notebook with handwritten verses and notes. He laughs, tries to play and sing one of the songs – but as he says, he does not know anything, and cannot play well at all. We are invited to eat at the home of a woman who has cooked for us, but we are not very hungry. Without much discussion it is decided that we will just eat later. The food for lunch would have been as usually corn, potato and cassava (which sometimes is accompanied with birds or animals that have been hunt). There is not need to hurry with anything. After a while, a guy suggests going for a swim, and – again without much discussion – everybody stands up to go to the nearby lagoon. They ask me if I would also like to join them there. I say "yes."

Outlook: Social Movements, Affective Scapes and Outside Politics

The various people to whom this volume refers are, on the one hand, "everyday people" in the sense in which DeCertau (1984) speaks of the "everyday man," (and woman) the average person, who usually history does not write about and who makes up the bulk of the population participating in the practice of everyday life. However, the people to whom this volume refers are radical Others to the average "everyday" men and women of the Brazilian middle classes – even of the ones who might perceive themselves as "subcultural." The young people I have studied above live in social spaces that are constituted by quite radical social movements. Sharing common goods, enjoying solidarity with each other, being threatened by dominant politics, and sometimes trying literally to survive are some of the aspects of their everyday lives that mark their Otherness to the Brazilian middle or upper classes.

These youths are not only *constituted by* but also *constitutive of* the social movements in question. Every time Carlos or Raquel manage to escape what can be seen as "expected" or "normal" from the point of view of average Brazilian people, they question the given power relations. But also precisely every time they manage to live their lives as "normal," experiencing feelings such as calmness, enthusiasm, or love, it appears that they un-do the margins in which they are placed (cf. Smolka, Magiolino-Salomão, dos Santos-Braga & Horta-Nogueira, this volume; Coracini, this volume). These young people constitute a *radical politics* that is the very essence of what can be seen as "movement" – be it the National Movement of the Struggle for Housing, the Landless Workers' Movement, the indigenous movements or the urban movements for education for all.

The young people, to whom this work refers, are also Others to each other ("Landless Rural Workers" youth are not urban "homeless" youth, who in turn are not "Guarani" youth). This is the reason I would hesitate to label all of them just as *oppressed* in the Freireian sense (Freire, 1986). It is quite interesting that the movements in question differ a lot from each other – although all of them take place in contemporary Brazil. They are heterogeneous regarding their forms of production and division of labor, kinship structures, their organization of time and space as well as their ways of perceiving and performing one's identity and difference to others. It is Marxism that *brings together* young people of very different ethnic and racial backgrounds in the context of the Landless Workers' Movement, while *ethnic identity* – being Guarani – is exactly what marks Otherness in what can be seen the indigenous movements. Knowledge on how to survive in one's territory, how to deal with the state and how to communicate with Others (entailing communication with other social movements) may vary a lot among these movements (cf. Caldart, Paludo & Doll, 2006; Cabalzar, 2012).

The "participation" of young people in constituting the social spaces they live in also varies across the different movements. For example one could say that the "homeless" young students are "hosted" at their schools, which are run by engaged teachers. The young people at the occupation in Porto Alegre, however, constitute the social space in which they live by themselves, in regard to all possible dimensions: negotiating with authorities, undertaking reparations/renovations, planning the spatial and temporal organization, dealing with food and hygiene.

Papadopoulos and colleagues have criticized the emphasis of the social sciences on *macro-politics* and later on *micro-politics* (Papadopoulos, Stephenson, & Tsianos, 2008; Stephenson & Papadopoulos, 2006). They suggest the use of the term *outside politics* to describe the everyday efforts – often self-evident or just driven by the desire to survive, without any particular theoretical aspiration – of the people who are "outside" of the current political, economical and societal organization to live their lives, not merely through entering the "inside" but through transforming the whole, through shifting the borders of the inside and the outside and transforming the inner organization of the inside. This "movement" or "politics" irreversibly transforms the cornerstones of the current political, economical, and societal organization, e.g. what is "democracy" is considered to be or who a "citizen" is.

According to Papadopoulos and colleagues, outside politics is *heterogeneous* – a collective emerges without any necessity that one participant becomes more like the others, and without any central organization that applies the same principles to every action. The approach of Papadopoulos and colleagues offers tools for understanding the everyday experience of the young people to whom this study refers as *single* and at the same time as *multiple* – which implies an emphasis on processes and not on structural differences.

The single and multiple aspects of everyday experience manifest themselves in the *affective scapes* in which the everyday lives of the young people unfold – and which I have tried to present in my ethnography. Arjun Appadurai in his *Modernity At Large* (1996) speaks about five different scapes: ethno-, media-, techno-, finance- and ideo- scapes, which offer a framework for examining the new global cultural economy of "complex, overlapping, amorphous, and disjunctive flows" of people, media images, capital, ideologies, and technologies that move across what could be seen as a "fixed" typical landscape and beyond any center-periphery divisions. Such complex, overlapping, amorphous, and disjunctive flows of people, media images, capital, ideologies, and technologies constitute contemporary "Brazil" as well as contemporary "Brazilian" critical research – after 50 years of complex, overlapping, amorphous, and disjunctive flows of theoretical concepts and research methodologies from "Brazil" to the "outside" and vice versa.

Thinking of my research with José, Carlos, Raquel, and Werá Mirim, as well as of the research projects presented in the previous book chapters, one could also add to Appadurai's conceptual framework the notion of *affective scapes* which are marked by intense emotional and affective qualities, are single and at the same time multiple – constituted by and constitutive of what can be seen as "youth in movement." According to Appadurai:

> [T]he individual actor is the last locus of this perspectival set of landscapes, for these landscapes are eventually navigated by agents who both experience and constitute larger formations, in part from their own sense of what these landscapes offer. (Appadurai, p. 33)

While moving the focus away from "individual actors" (here referring to "research participants" as well as to "researchers" or "practitioners"), exploring *affective scapes* condenses in a particular way and transcends at the same time the subjective and the collective; exploring *affective scapes* challenges conventional notions of "theory", "research", "practice", "intervention", "ideology" – and last but not least: of "writing". Instead of offering an epilogue to *Facing Poverty and Marginalization: 50 Years of Critical Research in Brazil* this last chapter invites indeed the reader to dive into fluid ethno-, media-, techno-, finance-, ideo- and affective scapes as to question and expand one's given conceptions and participate in the endless heterogeneous becoming (of) *youth in movement*.

Acknowledgements

I am very thankful to my Brazilian colleagues Maria Florentina Camerini, Maurício Canuto, Denise Comerlato, Johannes Doll, Gilton Mendes, Erineu Foerste, Gerda Margit Schütz Foerste, Ana Lopes, Marisol Barenco de Mello, Ozirlei Teresa Marcilino and Jackeline Rodrigues for collaborating with me during this research as described in footnote 1. Special thanks is also ought to the director, the teachers and students of Escola Porto Alegre as well as of the Centro Municipal d' Educação dos Trabalhadores in Porto Alegre. I also feel grateful to Bernd Fichtner, who helped me prepare my research before departing from Germany to Brazil the first time I was there. I am also very thankful to the young people to whom I refer above, and to all other people whom I met in my research fields, for the moments of loudness as well as for the moments of silence we shared. The funding of my research was covered indirectly through talks that I gave at Brazilian universities parallel to my fieldwork. I am very thankful to the

Catholic University of São Paulo, University of Taubaté, State University of Campinas, Federal University of Espírito Santo and Federal University of Rio Grande do Súl for inviting me – these invitations provided a very fruitful space, not only for discussion and exchange but also for collaborative research.

References

Appadurai, A. (1996). *Modernity at large: Cultural dimensions of globalization*. Minneapolis and London: University Of Minnesota Press.

Barreto A. (2005). *Terapia comunitária passo a passo*. Fortaleza: Gráfica LCR.

Cabalzar, F. D. (Ed.) (2012). *Educação escolar indígena do Rio Negro 1998–2011: Relatos de experiencias e liçoes aprendidas*. São Paulo & São Gabriel da Cachoeira: FOIRN/ISA.

Caldart, R. S., Paludo, C., & Doll, J. (2006). *Como se formam os sujeitos do campo? Idosos, adultos, jovens, crianças e educadores*. Brasília: PRONERA/NEAD.

Camini, I., & Kontopodis, M. (this volume). Educating in itinerancy: Countryside life and novel forms of schooling. In: M. Kontopodis, M. C. Magalhães, & M. J. Coracini (Eds), *Facing Poverty and Marginalization: Fifty Years of Critical Research in Brazil*. Oxford: Peter Lang.

Comerlato, D., Stumpf Buaes, C., & Pólvora (this volume). In: M. Kontopodis, M. C. Magalhães, & M. J. Coracini (Eds), *Facing Poverty and Marginalization: Fifty Years of Critical Research in Brazil*. Oxford: Peter Lang.

Coracini, M. J. (this volume). The Dis-order of discourse: Young people confined in CASA (São Paulo) and a poet considered insane in Colônia Juliano Moreira (Rio de Janeiro). In: M. Kontopodis, M. C. Magalhães, & M. J. Coracini (Eds), *Facing Poverty and Marginalization: Fifty Years of Critical Research in Brazil*. Oxford: Peter Lang.

da Silva, J. F. (2008). Escola Itinerante Paulo Freire: Experiência de educação *Cadernos da Escola Itinerante – MST*, 1(2), 7–24.

de Andrade, A. (2008). Escola Itinerante Sementes do Amanhã: Uma história de lutas e conquistas. *Cadernos da Escola Itinerante – MST*, 1(2), 25–42.

DeCerteau, M. (1984). *The Practice of Everyday Life* (S. R. Berkley, Trans.). Los Angeles and London: University of California Press.

Diniz-Pereira, J. E. (2005). Teacher education for social transformation and its links to progressive social movements: The case of the Landless Workers Movement in Brazil. *Journal for Critical Education Policy Studies*, 3(2), <http://www.jceps. com/?pageID=article&articleID=51>.

Emerson, R. M., Fretz, R. I., & Shaw, L. L. (2003). *Writing ethnographic fieldnotes*. Chicago: University of Chicago Press.

Farias, A. N. (2008). A trajetória de resistência da Escola Itinerante Ernest Che Guevara. *Cadernos da Escola Itinerante – MST*, 1(2), 43–64.

Faubion, J. D., & Marcus, G. E. (2009). *Fieldwork is not what it used to be: learning anthropology's method in a time of transition*. Ithaca: Cornell University Press.

Ferreira-Filha, M. O. & Dias M. D. (2006). *Terapia comunitária: Uma ação básica de saúde mental*. João Pessoa: Projeto de Extensão (PROBEX)/UFPB.

Freire, P. (1986). *Pedagogy of the oppressed*. New York: Continuum.

Foerste, E. (2004). *Professores sem-terra e universidade: Qual parceria?* Paper presented at the II Simpósio de Pesquisa em Educação.

Foerste, E. (2009). Pädagogik des Landes: Eine Qualitative Bewertung der Zusammenarbeit zwischen der "Bewegung Landloser Bauern" und der Universität. Universidade Federal do Espírito Santo.

Friebertshäuser, B. (2003). Das Andere im Spiegel des Eigenen: Probleme des Verstehens fremder Lebenswelten. In B. Fichtner, M. T. Freitas & R. Monteiro (Eds), *Kinder und Jugendliche im Blick qualitativer Forschung* (pp. 62–81). Oberhausen: Athena.

Hall, S., & Jefferson, T. (1976). *Resistance through rituals: Youth subcultures in post-war Britain*. London: Hutchinson.

Karriem, A. (2009). The rise and transformation of the Brazilian landless movement into a counter-hegemonic political actor: A Gramscian analysis. *Geoforum*, 40(3), 316–325.

Kontopodis, M. (Ed.). (2009). *Children, culture and emerging educational challenges: A dialogue with Brazil, Latin America*. Berlin: Lehmanns Media.

Marcus, G. E. (1986). Contemporary problems of ethnography in the modern world System. In J. Clifford & G. E. Marcus (Eds), *Writing culture: The poetics and politics of ethnography* (pp. 165–193). Berkeley: University of California Press.

Marcus, G. E. (1998). *Ethnography through thick and thin*. Princeton, NJ: Princeton University Press.

Papadopoulos, D., Stephenson, N., & Tsianos, V. (2008). *Escape routes: Control and subversion in the twenty-first century*. London: Pluto Press.

Pizetta, J. A., & Souza, A. P. (2005). Entre luta, esperança e utopia: A caminhada do MST no ES no Período de 1984 a 2005. In A. P. Souza, J. A. Pizetta, H. Gomes & D. Casali (Eds), *A reforma agrária e o MST no Espírito Santo* (pp. 73–146). Vitória: Secretaria Estadual Movimento Sem Terra.

Ribeiro, M. (2008). Pedagogia da alternância na educação rural/do campo: projetos em disputa. *Educação & Pesquisa*, 34(1), 27–45.

Rodrigues Mendes, J. (this volume). Indigenous children and identity politics: Numeracy Practices among the Kaiabi from Xingu, Mato Grosso. In: M. Kontopodis, M. C. Magalhães, & M. J. Coracini (Eds), *Facing Poverty and Marginalization: Fifty Years of Critical Research in Brazil*. Oxford: Peter Lang.

Smolka, A. L., Magiolino-Salomão, L., dos Santos-Braga, E. & Horta-Nogueira, A. L. (this volume). "Special" and "normal" in students' voices: Meaning production at a State-funded school in Campinas. In: M. Kontopodis, M. C. Magalhães, & M. J. Coracini (Eds), *Facing Poverty and Marginalization: Fifty Years of Critical Research in Brazil*. Oxford: Peter Lang.

Stephenson, N., & Papadopoulos, D. (2006). *Analysing everyday experience: Social research and political change*. London: Palgrave Macmillan.

Tangerino, C. C. (Ed.). (1996). *Comunidade indígena Guarani Tekoha Porã (ES). Revelações sobre a terra: a memória viva dos Guarani*. Vitória: Universidade Federal do Espírito Santo.

Taussig, M. T. (2004). *My cocaine museum*. Chicago: University of Chicago Press.

Taussig, M. T. (2006). *Walter Benjamin's grave*. Chicago: University of Chicago Press.

Tonkin, E. (2010). Writing up imaginatively: Emotions, temporalities and social encounters. *Outlines: Critical Practice Studies*, 2(1), 15–30.

Wulf, C., & Gebauer, G. (2010). Emotion – Bewegung – Körper. *Paragrana. Internationale Zeitschrift für Historische Anthropologie*, 19(1) (Special Issue).

Notes on Contributors

ELIZABETH DOS SANTOS BRAGA is Professor of Education at the School of Education of the University of São Paulo, Brazil. She received her master's and doctorate in educational science at the State University of Campinas, where she then became a member of the *Thought and Language* research group. She has also accomplished post-doctoral studies at the Oxford Centre for Sociocultural and Activity Theory Research, Department of Education, at the University of Oxford. Her publication and research interests concern social memory, discourse and narrative, human development, subject constitution, social practices, school practices, and teacher education. She is the author of the book *A Constituição Social da Memória: Uma Perspectiva Histórico-Cultural* (The Social Constitution of Memory: A Historico-Cultural Perspective, Editora Unijuí, 2000).

CAROLINE STUMPF BUAES obtained her master's and doctoral degrees from the School of Education at Federal University of Rio Grande do Sul, Porto Alegre. Her research interests and publications concern the education of adults and the elderly.

ISABELA CAMINI obtained her PhD in Educational Science in 2009 from the Federal University of Rio Grande do Sul. Since 1994 she has been a core member of the National Centre for the Education of the Landless Rural Workers. Currently she is dedicated to the systematization of pedagogical experiences at school – specifically at schools in encampments of the Landless Rural Workers' Movement. She coedited three special issues of the journal *Itinerant School Notebooks* with Sandra Dalmagro: "Itinerant: the Landless School – Trajectories and Meanings" (2008); "Researches about the Itinerant School: Reflecting the School Movement" (2009); and "Pedagogy constructed at Itinerancy: Orientations for Educators" (2009). She has also published the book *Escola Itinerante: Na Fronteira de uma Nova Escola* (Itinerant School: On the Frontier of a New School, Expressão Popular, 2009).

DENISE COMERLATO accomplished her master's and doctoral degrees in pedagogy at the School of Education of the Federal University of Rio Grande do Sul, where she now works as an associate professor. Her field of research is youth and adult education. She is the author of: *A Escola (In)visível* (The (In-)visible School, co-authored with M. Eizirik, Editora da UFRGS, 2004) and *Os Trajetos do Imaginário na Alfabetização de Adultos* (Trajectories of the Imaginary in Adults' Alphabetization, EDUCAT, 1998). She also participates as a researcher in the *Movimento de Luta pela Moradia* (Movement of Struggle for Housing) in Porto Alegre.

MARIA JOSÉ R. F. CORACINI holds a PhD in applied linguistics from the Pontifícia Universidade Católica de São Paulo (Brazil). She is a professor at the Department of Applied Linguistics at the Universidade Estadual de Campinas (UNICAMP). She is also a researcher of the Conselho Nacional de Desenvolvimento Científico e Tecnológico. Her research explores the links between identity, migration and reading and writing in mother tongues and foreign languages. She is editor or co-editor of more than ten books in Portuguese and the author of the books *A Celebração do Outro: Arquivo, Memória e Identidade* (The Celebration of the Other: Arquive, Memory and Identity, Campinas: Mercado de Letras, 2007); *Um Fazer Persuasivo: O Discurso Subjetivo da Ciência* (A Persuasive Doing: The Subjective Discourse of Science, Pontes & EDUC, 1991).

MICHALIS KONTOPODIS obtained his PhD from the Free University Berlin, Germany in 2007. He has recently joined the University of Sheffield as a Senior Lecturer having held post-doc positions as well as assistant and visiting professorships at Roehampton University, Humboldt University Berlin, University of Amsterdam, Pontifícia Universidade Católica de São Paulo, Jawaharlal Nehru University and City University of New York. His research focuses on youth development, marginalization and global issues – the present volume is his second edited work about Brazil, the previous one was the book *Children, Culture & Emerging Educational Challenges: A dialogue with Brazil* (Lehmanns Media, 2009). He is also author of the book *Neoliberalism, Pedagogy and Human Development* (Routledge, 2014).

MARIA CECILIA CAMARGO MAGALHÃES (PhD Virginia Polytechnic, US) is a professor at the Department of Applied Linguistics and Language Studies of the Pontifical Catholic University of São Paulo, Brazil. She research interests include: language, critical thinking, collaboration, and intervention-oriented research. She also conducts research on continuing teacher education within the theoretical frame of cultural-historical activity theory. She has published articles and book chapters in Brazil, UK, Spain, and Denmark, and is the editor of the book *A Formação do Professor como um Profissional Crítico* (Education of Teachers as Critical Professionals, Mercado de Letras, 2004).

LAVÍNIA LOPES SALOMÃO MAGIOLINO accomplished her master's and doctoral degrees in educational science at the Faculty of Education, State University of Campinas, where she defended her thesis *Human emotions and signification in a historical-cultural perspective of human development: A theoretical study of the work of Vygotsky*. Currently, she is engaged in post-doctoral research in the Social Psychology Program at the Pontifícia Universidade Católica de São Paulo and in the Conservatoire National de Arts et Metiers in Paris (supported by FAPESP – Fundação de Amparo à Pesquisa do Estado de São Paulo).

MÁRCIA APARECIDA AMADOR MASCIA is a professor at the post-graduate program in education at the Universidade São Francisco in the State of São Paulo, Brazil. She accomplished her doctoral studies in applied linguistics at UNICAMP (Universidade Estadual de Campinas), completing part of it in the Department of Curriculum and Instruction at the University of Wisconsin-Madison. Her research focuses on discourse and identity issues in education. She has also explored the divergence between oral languages and sign languages with regard to deaf students and recently been engaged in analysing discourses of exclusion and resistance in schools. She is the author of the book *Investigações Discursivas na Pós-Modernidade – uma Análise das Relações de Poder-Saber do Discurso Político Educacional* (Discursive Investigations in Postmodernity: An Analysis of the Relations of Power and Knowledge of the Political Educational Discourse, Mercado de Letras/FAPESP, 2003).

JACKELINE RODRIGUES MENDES obtained her master's and doctoral degrees in applied linguistics from the State University of Campinas, São Paulo. She is Professor of Education associated with the research groups "Voices in School: Culture and Identity in Socio-linguistically Complex Scenarios", and "Education, Language and Socio-Cultural Practices" at the State University of Campinas (UNICAMP). She has worked in projects of indigenous teacher education since 1990, in the states of Mato Grosso, Rondonia, and Roraima.

ANA LUCIA HORTA NOGUEIRA is an associate professor at São Paulo University, Ribeirão Preto, Brazil, where she teaches educational psychology on undergraduate and graduate levels. She received her master's and doctoral degrees in educational science and accomplished a post-doctoral degree in applied linguistics at the State University of Campinas. In the last years, she has developed research on teacher's work and psychological development as well as on literacy and child development, within a cultural-historical perspective.

JACQUELINE BRITTO PÓLVORA is an urban anthropologist who obtained her master's degree from the Federal University of Rio Grande do Sul, Porto Alegre, Brazil, and her PhD in social anthropology from the University of Texas at Austin. Her research interests and publications focus on the construction of race and racism, urban informality in poor countries, land rights and urban exclusion.

ANA LUIZA BUSTAMANTE SMOLKA is Professor of Education at the State University of Campinas. She graduated in philosophy from the Catholic University of Rio de Janeiro, received her MA from the University of Arizona, and completed her PhD in Education at the State University of Campinas in Brazil. She is presently the coordinator of the *Thought and Language Research Group* and has been developing research related to school practices, discourse, language acquisition and literacy, teacher education, memory, emotion, and imagination. She has served as Associate Director of the Faculty of Education (1996–2000), and Coordinator of the Graduate School (2000–2002) at her university and as the President of the International Society for Sociocultural Studies (1996–2000).

ELZIRA YOKO UYENO † held a PhD in applied linguistics from the University of Campinas (UNICAMP). She was a professor at the master's program in applied linguistics at the University of Taubaté (UNITAU), where she conducted research in the areas of discourse analysis, psychoanalysis, and deconstruction until she died a year ago. Her research focused on contemporary forms of subjectivity in relation to the discourse inside and outside the classroom. She also studied the processes of teaching and learning languages. She was editor of many books and special issues such as *Cognicao, Afetividade e Linguagem* (Cognition, Affectiveness and Language, Cabral, 2006) and *Avaliar, Corrigir e Comentar Redações, Subsídios para Formação Continuada* (Evaluating, Correcting and Discussing Issues of Continuous Education, Cabral, 2010).

Index

(POST)CRITICAL GLOBAL STUDIES

Edited by

Márcia Aparecida Amador Mascia,
Universidade São Francisco, Brazil

Silvia Grinberg
Universidad Nacional de General San Martín, Argentina

Michalis Kontopodis
University of Sheffield, UK

This book series focuses on critical and post-critical research in the broad area of social sciences. It aims to trace the stimulating exchange of ideas on contemporary social issues between Latin America and the rest of the world and to explore possibilities for local and global social change. Furthermore, the series aims to situate and possibly deconstruct the systems of reasoning that govern social problems and global change, including deconstructing Euro-American critical paradigms. The series encourages innovative theoretical and methodological approaches to emerging phenomena in fields such as urban and rural studies, indigenous studies, human rights, social policy and social movements, intersectionality, media and technology, education, community organization, political economy, ecology, migration and globalization. It will discuss issues such as the geopolitics of knowledge, Paulo Freire's legacy and post-Freirean approaches, feminisms in Latin America and other areas of the majority world, anthropologies of the state and civil society, and de-/post-colonial perspectives, among others.

The series will include publications in English, Spanish and/or Portuguese. It is addressed to social scientists from Latin America and all over the world as well as to global policy makers and employees at international organizations and NGOs who are interested in theoretical and methodological innovation in social studies.

Vol. 1   Michalis Kontopodis, Maria Cecilia Magalhães and Maria José Coracini (eds)
Facing Poverty and Marginalization: Fifty Years of Critical Research in Brazil.
2016. ISBN 978-1-906165-64-2